# THE NEW FARM

# THE NEW FARM

## CONTEMPORARY RURAL ARCHITECTURE

DANIEL P. GREGORY

PRINCETON ARCHITECTURAL PRESS   NEW YORK

Contents

# FOREWORD

Abby Rockefeller

"Where there is no beauty, there is great danger," William Coperthwaite wrote in his 2002 book *A Handmade Life: In Search of Simplicity*. American culture itself is in danger. With the abandonment of a fundamental commitment to sustainable scale and the mad pursuit of "efficiency" and profit, beauty has been dropped by the wayside.

A way of feeling this crisis is to see that the "culture" has been removed from the word *agriculture*. *Agri* means, in Latin, "of the field," and *culture*, from the Latin *cultura*, means "care of." Thus *agriculture* means "care of the field"—care of the soil. This "care of the soil" means one thing especially: putting and keeping the carbon in the soil. Carbon is the backbone of humus, and humus is the sine qua non of healthy soil.

So what happened to strip agriculture in the United States of its culture? The driver has been corporate-based economics. Through the commodification of food and the consolidation of farmland under corporate control, our food system has been appropriated for the sake of profit. Our small-scale farmers—one by one, ten by ten, a thousand by a thousand—went under. The larger the farm, the lower the cost of production and the greater the profits for corporate agriculture—accomplished largely by eliminating the costs of caring for the soil.

The rationale for this displacement was that the sting of poverty in America would be lessened by "affordable" food. But scale matters greatly, though the concept of economies of scale has nothing to do with the right scale. There is a right scale, or right range of scales, for every kind of farming. When the scale is right for the purpose—when it is good for the farm family, good for the animals, and good for the land—there is beauty.

We struggle to find the words for this. *Sustainable* is one such word. It means that there is a balance on the farm that can be maintained indefinitely without ruining the soil, the people, the animals, or the ecosystem in which the farm is embedded. It means that on a dairy farm, for example, there is a small enough number of cows—fifteen to thirty-five rather than two hundred to two thousand—so that the farm family can get the manure on the land in a timely and appropriate manner. It means that the family can treat all of the animals with the care that they, as living creatures, need and deserve. It means that the family can tend the farm without feeling continually at wit's end performing the ceaseless work required to satisfy a rapacious economy.

In the late 1800s and the first half of the 1900s, there were brave and prescient souls who understood the necessary conditions for agriculture of scale, sustainability, and beauty. Albert Howard, Eve Balfour, Rudolf Steiner, and J. I. Rodale were among these. The term *organic farming*, conceived by these early heroes of real agriculture (the sort with the "culture" in it), was intended to stress the primary importance of the humus (and its carbon) in the soil. Only secondarily did it refer to the importance of not using poisons to deal with pests and diseases. The word *organic* refers to carbon, which refers to life. Wherever there is carbon there is, or was, life.

Organic agriculture, taken seriously, is the kind of agriculture that nurtures the soil, possessing both sustainability and beauty. There is a growing awareness among both young and old that all the processes compatible with life—with generation and re-generation—have beauty. We must order the fundamental practices of our existence so that they are compatible with life. The growing of food should not be for profit, any more than education or health care should be for profit. All should contribute to good livings and good lives.

Small is indeed beautiful in the world of agriculture. The family farm has been a wholesome cell in the body of the human community; this book is a strong—and beautiful—response to a century of destruction of beauty in agriculture.

*Abby Rockefeller is the founder of the Churchtown Dairy.*

# INTRODUCTION:
# WHAT IS
# A NEW FARM?

Gregory Farm,
Santa Cruz
Mountains,
California,
drawing by
William Wurster,
ca. 1927

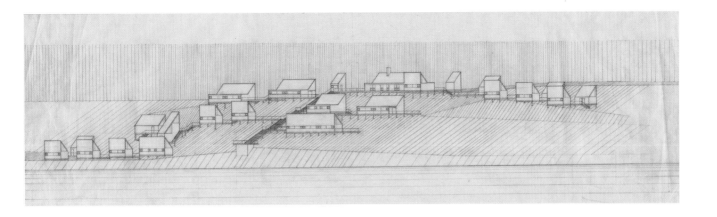

Haystack Mountain School of Crafts, Deer Isle, Maine, oblique elevation by Edward Larrabee Barnes, 1962

The farm is as old as civilization, but what is a new, or modern, farm? E. B. White's Zuckerman farm in *Charlotte's Web* is modern in that it's where, thanks to the precocious spider Charlotte, "Some Pig!" Wilbur gets raised not for sausage but celebrity. My grandparents' California farm in the Santa Cruz Mountains south of San Francisco is modern in that it was a real farm that became a weekend retreat noted for the farmhouse designed by architect William Wurster in 1927, an early example of the Bay Region Style in architecture. The harvest there was, and is, relaxation. My room was the lookout at the top of the water tower, which inspired my lifelong interest in buildings and perhaps inevitably led me to this topic. But this book is about the architecturally modern working farm.

The words *modern* and *farm* have long been associated with contemporary architectural developments because both suggest concepts of functionalism, simplicity, and practicality. As the exemplars of farm architecture, barns especially have provided architectural inspiration. For example, twentieth-century ranch house popularizer Cliff May, whose career spanned the 1930s through the 1970s, with more than eighteen thousand designs to his credit, once said, "The barn is made to spend not a nickel more than you need to house the horse or the cow or the feed.... You never see a bad barn!"[1]

New York architect Edward Larrabee Barnes, who worked briefly for Wurster right after World War II, designed the award-winning Haystack Mountain School of Crafts on Deer Isle, Maine, in 1961, as a collection of shed-roofed, shingle-sided cottages and studios—as if one very large barn had been sliced into modules and scattered among trees and granite outcroppings along a dramatic site sloping down to the ocean. He said, in a 1989 interview with *Architecture* magazine, "I've always been drawn to making things as simple as possible if you can do that without making them inhuman or dull or oppressive."[2] And San Francisco architect Joseph Esherick, whose firm designed the Monterey Bay Aquarium as well as museums, colleges, and houses, often asked himself as he started a new design, "How would a farmer do it?"[3]

Built on the site of several former sheep ranches, the 1964 Sea Ranch community on California's Sonoma County coast preserved several existing barns, and the original designers—including Esherick, MLTW Architects (Charles Moore, Donlyn Lyndon, William Turnbull Jr., and Richard Whitaker), and landscape architect Lawrence Halprin—used them as idea generators. By manipulating and abstracting details like exposed timber frames and vertical board walls, they created a lively dialogue with the site and its agrarian history, as you can see in the interior elevation of Charles Moore's own loftlike unit in Sea Ranch Condominium One. Or, as Lyndon told me, "We didn't want to make it look like a barn, but we wanted it to have the presence of a barn."[4]

Building on that design heritage, William Turnbull designed a barnlike but sculpturally abstract modern winery for Jack and Dolores Cakebread, in Rutherford, California,

Sea Ranch, Sonoma
County, California,
Black Point Barn
and Condominium
One, 1965

Sea Ranch,
Condominium One,
interior elevation
by William Turnbull,
1965

VIEW LOOKING NORTH

UNIT 1

UPPER FLOOR PLAN

GROUND FLOOR PLAN

Cakebread Cellars,
Rutherford, California,
designed by William
Turnbull, with Ross
Anderson, 1983–94

beginning in 1983. Many years ago I attended a dinner there, surrounded by multistoried racks of oak barrels and the heady scent of maturing Chardonnay and Sauvignon Blanc. There were about forty of us at one long table in the central aisle under the main gable. Toasting accelerated as the wine flowed. The low light, warm-toned wood, and tall, nave-like space added to the sense that this was a devotional exercise. By the end of the meal, most eyes were wet with emotion. Structure and sustenance come together at Cakebread Cellars to create an especially memorable experience.

It's clear that the farm has come to modern architecture, but has modern architecture come to the farm? Yes—and in one case, by sea! It's a project by Vermont-based McLeod Kredell Architects. Over the course of one week in Maine, John McLeod and his team designed and built a farm stand, compost station, shed, movable chicken coops (also called tractors), and a greenhouse "on a rugged, off-the-grid base camp island, then loaded them on a boat, transported them to their permanent sites on neighboring islands, and installed them," explains McLeod. The clients were a community school in Islesboro and another at North Haven, on the island of Vinalhaven, both expanding their farm practice curricula. These physically expressive, rough-board structures, shown on the following pages, are designed to withstand exposure to the harsh coastal climate throughout the year and to perform multiple functions.

For example, the farm stand also serves as a billboard, band shell, and sheltered deck. The compost station (with its own small deck) becomes an outdoor classroom. The shed accommodates farmers' market tables and concessions for community events. The eye-catching chicken tractors, which resemble long, barrel-chested sleds, are designed to be portable by two high school students so the broiler chickens can "root around

Farm structures on Maine's Islesboro and Vinalhaven islands, 2013–15, part of Island Design Assembly, a workshop run by McLeod Kredell Architects

different parts of the farm every other day, including being placed over row crops at the end of the season for the chickens to grub," according to McLeod, and double as garden seating for student workers. The greenhouse serves as a garden classroom and potting shed for elementary school students. For his designs, McLeod says he drew inspiration from "the simple yet iconic structures of the Maine coast: sheds, barns, boathouses, lobster traps, sailboats, and lighthouses."

The idea of the barn is always present in the modern farm, but often reimagined. In Somis, California, fifty-five miles northwest of Los Angeles, a region known for avocados and oranges, architect Zoltan Pali designed a hay barn to store and feed his client's horses.

He combined what he calls the "modernist rigor" of a twelve-by-twelve-foot structural steel system with a more *wabi sabi*, "beauty in imperfection" approach: using hay bales to clad part of the barn. The horse stalls are enclosed in horizontally patterned wood panels; the bales stack on a shelf that rings the barn's exterior under a broad, flat overhang. "In winter the hay is green," he says, "but as the season unfolds it turns yellow." And the stacking pattern changes as the bales are used and replaced, giving the barn an arresting, ever-changing character. The simple and ingenious design makes this barn feel indigenous and contemporary at the same time.

Sometimes a barn is just a barn, but elegant detailing makes it stand out as an artful riff on the simple gabled barn idea, as in this 820-square-foot Elk Valley, Oregon, tractor shed by Fieldwork Design & Architecture, of Portland.

The standing-seam metal roof extends down the sides of the gable to become the walls as well. The sliding barn door is composed of vertical wood strips, as if the

metal seams have metamorphosed into wood. Clearly an equipment shed, the design also shows how one detail can turn an ordinary shape into something memorable. As the opening line of an article in *Sunset* magazine said about a home remodeling: "It's the same, only different."[5]

The term *architecturally modern working farm* might make you think that we are talking about a sort of agricultural International Style or the farm as factory. However, that would be too specific to the 1920s, the era highlighted by the Museum of Modern Art's famous 1932 exhibition *Modern Architecture: International Exhibition*, which focused on the modernism of Walter Gropius, Mies van der Rohe, and Le Corbusier, among others. Instead, though the farms in this book certainly have International Style DNA, we are defining *modern* more broadly, to encompass a wide range of architectural idioms as well as practices of organic farming and sustainability.

A lot has been happening in this world. Historian Gregory A. Barton, author of *The Global History of Organic Farming*, traces the popular rise of organic farming to 1980, when the US Department of Agriculture issued a major report on the subject, defining it as "a production system which avoids or largely excludes the use of synthetically compounded fertilizers, pesticides, growth regulators, and livestock feed additives. To the maximum extent feasible, organic farming systems rely on crop rotations, crop residues, animal manures, legumes, green manures, off-farm organic wastes, mechanical cultivations, mineral-bearing rocks, and aspects of biological pest control to maintain soil productivity and tilth to supply plant nutrients and to control insects, weeds, and other pests."

According to Barton, that report "for the first time brought the organic farming movement out of the cold, and though continued progress proved fitful, the organic farming movement grew exponentially in the United States, and increasingly, around the world."[6] The farms in this book are not large-scale examples of agribusiness but more intimate family enterprises that combine organic approaches with modern design sensibilities.

One of the most illustrative examples of an old farm embracing new ideas is the nonprofit Stone Barns Center for Food & Agriculture in Pocantico Hills, New York, which was originally designed as a dairy for the John D. Rockefeller Jr. family by Beaux-Arts-trained New York architect Grosvenor Atterbury and completed in 1933.

The original core of Stone Barns Center includes a horse stable, hay barn, cow barn, silos, garages, and offices on eighty rolling acres. The inspiration for Atterbury's picturesque complex of tawny stone, red brick, and half-timbering with slate roofs was French Norman architecture. A lower-level arcade supports an upper-level courtyard

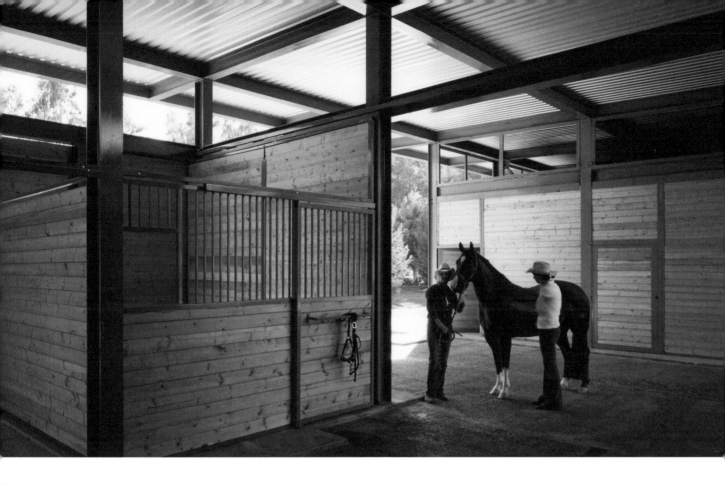

Hay Barn, Somis,
California, Zoltan
Pali Architects,
2004

Elk Valley, Oregon,
tractor shed,
Fieldwork Design &
Architecture, 2014

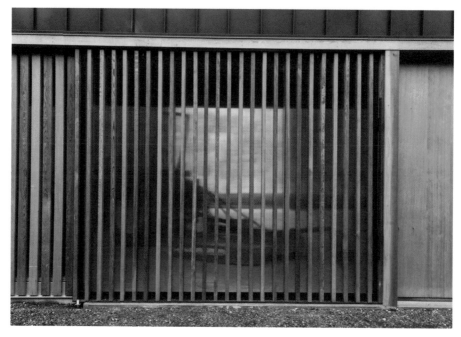

Stone Barns Center
for Food and
Agriculture, Pocantico
Hills, New York, master
plan by Machado
Silvetti Architects,
2000–2004

dominated by an imposing three-story hay barn and round silos on the northwest, with a distinctive stone-and-timber entry on the southwest. Today, the complex, which was restored and master-planned by the architecture firm Machado Silvetti between 2000 and 2004, houses offices, a cafe, and a store, while the hay barn has been refurbished as an event venue.

The former cow barn and manure shed now house Blue Hill at Stone Barns, founded by chef Dan Barber, his brother, David Barber, and his sister-in-law, Laureen Barber. The elegant design of the restaurant, by Laureen and Asfour Guzy Architects, is the result of exposing and burnishing the details: stone, timbers, and steel trusses as well as new connections to patios and courtyards. There are no menus; instead, guests are offered what's best from the surrounding fields and pastures and from other local farms at that moment. Indeed, a meal at Blue Hill is a memorable riff on "a movable feast," with small bites enjoyed in a series of locations throughout the restaurant.

Approximately half of what is produced at Stone Barns Center is sold to the restaurant, and the rest is distributed through their CSA (Community Supported Agriculture) program, sold in the store, or used in their education and public programming. Blue Hill cooks participate in the harvest. The approach at Stone Barns Center is to take into account the entire ecosystem: not just the 350 varieties of vegetables grown on, say, one experimental plot, but also a seven-year crop rotation and what kind of runoff is being generated. Stone Barns Center provides a wide array of educational experiences as well as fresh produce, meat, and eggs for farm-to-table meals.

Peggy Dulany, a daughter of David and Peggy Rockefeller, started Stone Barns Center with her father to make an educational campus for meaningful agricultural work and to honor her mother, who started the American Farmland Trust in 1980 to protect family farms. She raised Simmental cattle—and thereby hangs a tale. Dulany's sister Eileen writes in her engrossing memoir, *Being a Rockefeller, Becoming Myself*, that when their parents were invited to visit the king of Morocco in the early 1980s, they thought long and hard about a gift to bring. Their mother decided to give the king one of her prize bulls. The king was already sending three jets to the United States to pick up spare parts for his air fleet, so he diverted one to Stewart Air Force base in New York. "In the end they had to jettison a spare engine…just to be able to fit the bull and his crate on the plane."[7]

As industrial-scale farming has become more efficient and reliant on technology to plant, protect, and harvest, the farmer has become less connected to the land. Stone Barns Center is all about reversing this trend, as it follows a strong philosophy of sustainability and trains new farmers while educating the public in "agro-ecological" practices. A good example is its use of the recently developed Oggun tractor, which

The pottery studio
at Chiltern Barns,
Buckinghamshire,
England, McLean
Quinlan, 2015

At Chiltern
Barns, the
new structure
encloses
the original
courtyard.

is cleverly designed with off-the-shelf parts and is made to be fixed in the field or in a local shop. Developed by Cuban-born software engineer Saul Berenthal and his business partner, Horace Clemmons (*oggun* is a Cuban term meaning "iron horse"), it is small enough to roll along a row of crops. Such tools allowing easy use and maintenance can make it possible for small farms to operate in metropolitan areas. According to Stone Barns Center senior communications manager Jessica Galen, the idea is to "let the farmer drive the technology" and not the other way around.

About an hour and a quarter northwest of London, near High Wycombe in Buckinghamshire (not far from the manor house that was once the residence of Prime Minister Benjamin Disraeli), is an especially appealing modern riff on the agricultural compound: Chiltern Barns. Architects Fiona McLean, Kate Quinlan, and Alastair Bowden (of London- and Winchester-based McLean Quinlan) were asked to expand an existing brick stable for alpaca, chickens, pigs, and sheep and add a pottery studio.

They did so by sharpening and extending the stable's existing U shape with new buildings tucked into a slope and clad in vertical cedar boards and tawny brick. The new structures follow the ridge height and gable profile of the original stable and accentuate the symmetry of its layout.

An elegant brick wall wraps around the new buildings and encloses the courtyard. The hue echoes the color of the wood siding and works as a foil to the original brick stable block, now painted black. The contrast articulates the design's innovative balance of old and new. An opening in the center of the wall lines up with the residence some distance away. The completed compound reads as a small modern stockade—for animals and people. A good stockade should have a lookout, and here it's the pottery studio in one corner of the addition, with its large window onto the rolling landscape and passing alpacas, no doubt eager to see what pots are currently being thrown.

A four-hour drive east of Vancouver, British Columbia, lies the dramatic conifer-studded Okanagan Valley. In Kelowna, hugging a steep hillside overlooking Okanagan Lake, is Martin's Lane Winery, designed by architect Tom Kundig, FAIA, RIBA, of Olson Kundig for von Mandl Family Estates to produce the highest quality Pinot Noir and Riesling. It is a memorably modern wine farm.

Wine grapes are dependent on terroir—the environmental conditions, especially soil and climate, that give a wine its unique character. But here the winery building itself expresses a sort of architectural terroir or geological abstraction: the strong diagonal form encased in rusty steel mimics the site's steep slope and resembles an exposed mineshaft or ski jump. Kundig explains: "The building is conceived as a rectangular form with a central split or 'fracture' down the middle, with the production side of the building following the direction of the site and the visitor area cantilevering out toward the horizon." A grand band of clerestory windows brings daylight into the production areas. Winemaker Anthony von Mandl describes how Kundig—a friend since they first worked together in 2001—brought his vision to life "in a contemporary design that totally reflects the rugged, intense natural environment of the Okanagan Valley. The corrugated, weathered Corten steel mirrors the bark of the surrounding ponderosa pines, and the black steel accents the blackened tree trunks scarred in a devastating forest fire that engulfed the region in 2003."

The design takes advantage of the slope for organizing wine production around gravity flow, which von Mandl says is essential for producing the highest-quality Pinot: "The skins are thin and extremely delicate and, to make exceptional wine, require the gentlest winemaking possible, and that means *no* mechanical pumping."

Grapes arrive at the top, and crushing and fermentation occur on successive levels (there are six), with barrel storage in a monumental hall below ground at the bottom.

Kundig says, "There's a beauty in the function and process of winemaking, and the building clearly expresses that function." I would go a step further: gravity flow reinforces the idea that the building itself is a nature-oriented architectural machine. Indeed, it is perhaps the largest of the sculptural inventions that Kundig has become famous for: his line of bespoke hardware and home furnishings as well as his marvelous oversized hand cranks for windows and doors, which evoke the work of Russian constructivist Vladimir Tatlin.

You could say that Stone Barns Center, Chiltern Barns, and Martin's Lane Winery represent architectural extremes: traditions revived, combined, and reinvented. What follows in this book are paradigms that show many other approaches that a modern farm can take, in the United States, Canada, Europe, and Australia. Think of it as an agricultural/architectural travelogue. So climb on that Oggun—or alpaca—or follow the gravity flow and explore!

Unless otherwise noted, quotes throughout the book are from personal communication between speaker and the author.

1   "The California Ranch House, Cliff May, Interviewed by Marlene L. Laskey," Oral History Program, University of California, Los Angeles, 1984, 30.
2   Quoted in Douglas Martin, "Edward Larrabee Barnes, Modern Architect, Dies at 89," *New York Times*, September 23, 2004.
3   Quoted in Daniel Gregory, "Joseph Esherick," in *Toward a Simpler Way of Life: The Arts & Crafts Architects of California*, ed. Robert Winter (Berkeley: University of California Press, 1997), 266.

4   Donlyn Lyndon, conversation with the author, January 21, 2019, about *The Sea Ranch: Architecture, Environment, and Idealism*, the exhibition organized by Jennifer Dunlop Fletcher and Joseph Becker for the San Francisco Museum of Modern Art, December 22, 2018–April 28, 2019.
5   "More Gables Outside, Much More Spaciousness Inside," *Sunset*, January 1990, 74.
6   Gregory A. Barton, *The Global History of Organic Farming* (Oxford: Oxford University Press, 2018), 188.
7   Eileen Rockefeller, *Being a Rockefeller, Becoming Myself* (New York: Blue Rider Press, 2013), 144.

At Martin's Lane,
production levels
descend the slope
to the barrel room
at the bottom.

Soter Vineyards,
Mineral Springs Ranch

Willamette Valley, Oregon

Simple outlines
frame serene views
at Oregon's Soter
Vineyards.

At Soter Vineyards, part of the 250-acre Mineral Springs Ranch and known for its Pinot Noir and Chardonnay, the tasting room occupies an especially compelling site on a vine-covered knoll overlooking the diverse farmsteads of the Willamette Valley in central Oregon. It's the main public-oriented feature but just part of an eloquent architectural ensemble designed by Howard Backen of Napa Valley's Backen & Gillam Architects, with his associate Luke Wade (now practicing on his own). The approach road, just off the two-lane state highway, leads through a flat field—recently plowed when I visited—and offers a view of the hill in the distance with several indistinct structures at the top.

The road curves around the back of the hill through tall stands of oak and fir. The working winery compound swings into view first: on the left is a large existing Dutch gambrel vehicle barn with walls covered in board-and-batten siding, an example of the local vernacular. Its standing-seam metal roof supports a line of solar panels. Beside it, on the right, is the new building where the wine is made and stored. Tucked into the hill, this shed-roofed structure also sports board-and-batten siding and a standing-seam metal roof and reads as a simplified extension of the original barn. Then, after one more curve, the road arrives at the crest in a small parking area.

It's a picturesque approach, like something the eighteenth-century English land-scape designer Lancelot "Capability" Brown might have composed—first offering a glimpse of the objective, then obscuring it before the sudden arrival face-to-face with the archetypal gable-roofed, board-and-batten barn following the ridge of the hill. On closer inspection, the structure appears restored or perhaps modernized: running the length of the building ridge is a monitor roof, its clerestory windows glinting in the sun-light. At each end are four symmetrical metal chimney vents; ahead is the entry, shel-tered under the broad overhang.

Now, as you walk forward, you see that the entry is not a door but a grand, pale-green, steel-and-glass window wall. It pivots up and out of the way, drawing you through the big room—with its concrete floor, open kitchen, and tasting bar on the left and dining/living area on the right—and through large glass sliding doors to a wide covered terrace and the view back over the valley you just traversed. The big room is symmetrical, with chimneys at each end (one for the fireplace and one for the range hood), recalling classical Georgian manor houses. And yet everything is contemporary: the exposed steel trusses, rows of skylights, and rolling glass barn doors. The board-and-batten siding covers interior walls as well, reinforcing the outdoor feeling. In short, it is both a barn and a modern indoor-outdoor room for entertaining, an artful melding of that original barn and barrel room down the hill.

Though owners Tony and Michelle Soter (he's a longtime wine grower, and her expertise is in advertising and marketing) had first planned to build one main house, they eventually asked Backen to design two guest houses nearby, one of which is where they live when they come to the vineyard from their main residence in Portland. Michelle was "keen to tuck auxiliary buildings into groves of trees to reduce the visual impact as

The winery at Soter, above, is built into the hill. The site plan shows how the various buildings straddle a rolling landscape. The outdoor-oriented tasting room stands apart from, and well above, the winery and caves.

well as deconstruct common functions by separating sleeping accommodations from community areas." These rustic-contemporary gable-roofed cabins are deftly sited on a boardwalk that follows a contour at the edge of the hill. They are visible from the tasting barn but far enough removed to preserve a sense of privacy. Tasting barn, boardwalk, and cabins form an elemental but powerful architectural frame that brings landscape views into focus: a hilltop rooted in the past and reaching toward the future.

Indeed, that was the Soters' objective. They wanted to become stewards of the land for generations and build a sustainable enterprise based on organic and biodynamic agriculture. In addition to cultivating grapes, they farm several acres of vegetables and raise meat birds, hogs, cattle, and goats. Twenty-five acres currently grow organic grains for animal feed. They turned to Backen & Gillam because they admired what Tony calls Backen's "aesthetic that honored traditional rural American architectural forms" that were also infused "with refinement, exceptional flexibility, and livability. We knew we wanted things to look as though they had been here for a very long time. Barn forms were natural." Were there any surprises? No, says Tony, except for "the realization that the vision we have will take decades to actualize. But then again, that's the journey." Well said, and true for any farmer, traditional or modern.

SOTER VINEYARDS, MINERAL SPRINGS RANCH

# Snuck Farm

Pleasant Grove, Utah

Snuck Farm, in Pleasant Grove, Utah, about forty minutes south of Salt Lake City along Interstate 15, is what you might call "Camouflage Ag." The 3.5-acre plot is surrounded on three sides by a nondescript subdivision of single-family homes with prominent street-facing garages. The farm is not open to the public, and the driveway is discreet, so, as owner Page Westover mentioned to me, even now, some neighbors are surprised to be told "You have a farm in your backyard!"

History explains the oddity: this densely planned acreage at the base of the Wasatch Mountains—with animal and equipment barns, a demonstration kitchen, offices, and large greenhouses for hydroponically raised arugula, kale, and butter lettuce—was built on what's left of a large hay and corn homestead planted by Westover's forebears, who were among Pleasant Grove's original settlers. Over the years the family sold off most of the real estate until Page decided to become a farmer.

Westover's grandfather Boyd Leroy Fugal, who first farmed the land, was known as a prankster in his youth and nicknamed "Snuck," which Westover and her family decided should be the name of the reinvented business. Westover, who trained as a nutritionist and worked for a children's hospital for ten years, loved the idea of taking a modern approach to agriculture: "Snuck Farm grew out of a desire to offer a different kind of life for my family. I wanted to provide them with a slower, more intentional way of living while interacting with the natural environment." The commitment to community is in her DNA: her father, Guy, was elected mayor of Pleasant Grove in 2018. The Fugal family businesses include pipeline construction and telecommunications. "In my life," she says, "I've been given the gift of opportunity. I feel inspired to use these opportunities to do something bigger than myself, with the hope that my children will observe my life, as I've observed my parents' and grandparents', and desire the same thing for themselves, their families, and their communities."

For the design of the new farm, Westover and her family turned to architectural designer Louise Hill and architect Warren Lloyd, both in Salt Lake City. Westover requested that one side of the barn be for living, with a commercial kitchen, and that the other be reserved for animals, including alpacas and chickens. The siting of the barn separates the pasture from the barnyard and greenhouses. Hill recalls, "My hope was to have the barn look like it had been there for years and the suburbs had grown up around it." Guy Fugal also requested a drive-through breezeway for large vehicles between the commercial kitchen on the west and the horse stalls on the east, which ultimately gave the project its organizing north–south axis. The result is a monumental passage that frames views into and out of the barnyard and, as Lloyd says, "orients on Lone Peak on the north and Mount Nebo on the south, anchoring the farm in the center of the Utah Valley."

The timber frame design combines rustic forms and materials: tall gable roofs over the central aisles, sheds over the saddlebag-like side aisles, reclaimed wood and

locally quarried stone, and board-formed concrete for the walls. The barn and breezeway act as the distribution center for Snuck Farm's CSA.

Across the barnyard is a separate hydroponics building constructed by Nexus, a company that specializes in state-of-the-art greenhouses. A roll-up airlock door prevents pest infiltration, along with the use of biological soaps and sprays and beneficial insects. Eighty percent of the greens that Snuck Farm produces are sold wholesale to the cafeterias of the region's burgeoning tech corridor, which includes such companies as Adobe, eBay, Thumbtack, and Vivint.

Snuck Farm is evolving as both a family enclave and a brand. The loft above the kitchen will eventually become Westover's office, but for now it's where her fourteen-year-old daughter practices the drums. And there is the realization that a farmer usually has something to barter: Westover and her team receive a once-a-week yoga class in return for providing a steady supply of salad greens—a healthy stretch all around!

Snuck Farm, south of Salt Lake City, reworks traditional barn forms.

The cross-axial main barn opens to both the driveway by the fence and the central courtyard by garage and greenhouses.

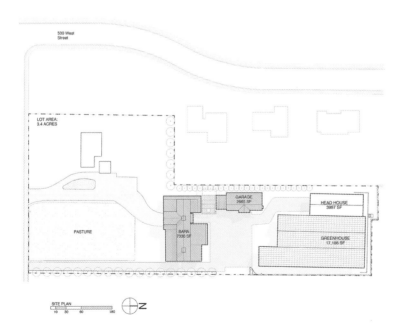

Snuck Farm owner Page Westover says most of her greens go to the cafeteria kitchens at tech companies in and around Lehi, Utah.

# Good Shepherd Poultry Ranch

Lindsborg, Kansas

The 160-acre Good Shepherd Poultry Ranch is near the tiny Swedish enclave of Lindsborg, Kansas, out on the open prairie, three hours west of Kansas City, at the very center of the state. Driving there means passing Topeka, then Abilene, home of the Dwight D. Eisenhower presidential library, and finally turning south at Salina for another forty minutes. As I swung into the dirt driveway, a large, friendly, buff-hued female mastiff suddenly appeared beside the car, loping along jauntily. As I got out and walked up to the barnyard gate, she presented her head to be scratched. She provided a delightful introduction to what I can only describe as an Oz of heritage turkeys and chickens and a remarkable poultry wizard named Frank Reese.

Now in his early seventies and a fourth-generation farmer, Reese has always loved poultry but started raising birds full-time only after serving in the army and working for years as a registered nurse anesthetist—because his father said he had to earn some money before he went into poultry farming. Unlike typical commercial turkeys and chickens, Good Shepherd birds are not artificially inseminated and receive no antibiotics. Their bloodlines go back a long way. The turkey breeds include Bronze (the original Thanksgiving turkey) and the rare White Holland. As Maryn McKenna writes in her influential 2017 book *Big Chicken: The Incredible Story of How Antibiotics Created Modern Agriculture and Changed the Way the World Eats*, Reese's farm "is a living archive of history and genetics, preserved because the birds bring him joy—and also because he believes, in defiance of the trends of decades, that the poultry industry erred in sacrificing them, and will someday need them again." As Reese himself tells me, "These chickens and turkeys have healthy immune systems."

Three large, long, metal-skinned, gable-roofed sheds border the poultry yard; twin feed silos are the main vertical landmark at one end. Reese built everything himself except for the two-story Victorian farmhouse, his home, near the road. It is a singular sensation to stand in the middle of the open space between the structures and be surrounded by five thousand seemingly very relaxed and friendly turkeys as they amble around. Reese quietly relates that he has been on Martha Stewart's television program twice and knows Berkeley chef-restaurateur-author Alice Waters—and that *New York Times* food columnist Marian Burros chose a Good Shepherd bird as the best-tasting turkey in America. In one of the sheds, he introduced me to twenty-five hundred chickens—including Delawares, Jersey Giants, and Cornish. Amid the racket of squawking he turned to me and said, "They are making so much noise because they don't know you." Whereupon, at the sound of his voice, they quieted a little, making me think that a good anesthetist never loses his bedside manner.

Kansas poultry whisperer Frank Reese is a calming influence on his heritage chickens and turkeys, which have pleased the palates of such food luminaries as Alice Waters and Martha Stewart. His operation also provides the natural fertilizer for cropland in the vicinity.

Good Shepherd
Poultry Ranch
in Kansas is
becoming a modern
agricultural
conservancy with
the help of MASS
Design.

Reese's organic approach is part of a larger goal, which is to establish the Good Shepherd Conservancy, whose mission is to "preserve and protect biodiversity through a unique model of agricultural education, ecological resilience, and food system innovation." Designed by Boston-based MASS Design Group and now under development, the modern wedge-shaped structure will include an archive/library, visitor center, experiment station, classrooms, and teaching kitchen. Reese showed me the site, on a slight rise, just beyond the chicken barn. I saw how the new building will transform a heritage operation into an innovative poultry university—a truly modern farm.

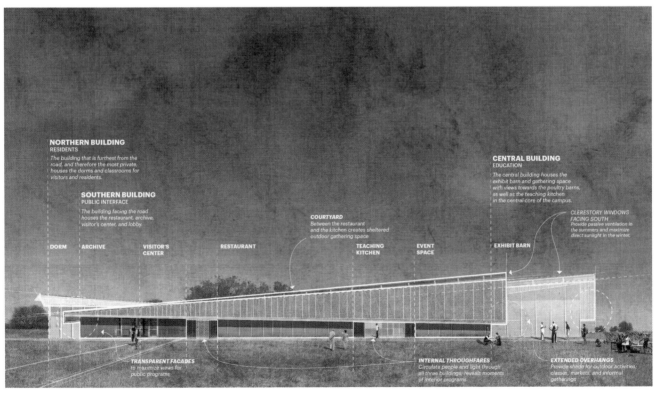

1. NATIVE PRAIRIE
2. CROPS
3. BUFFALO WALLOWS
4. POULTRY BARNS
5. FRANK'S HOUSE
6. STORAGE
7. INCUBATION BARN
8. DUCK POND

**NORTHERN BUILDING**
RESIDENTS
*The building that is furthest from the road, and therefore the most private, houses the dorms and classrooms for visitors and residents.*

**SOUTHERN BUILDING**
PUBLIC INTERFACE
*The building facing the road houses the restaurant, archive, visitor's center, and lobby.*

**COURTYARD**
*Between the restaurant and the kitchen creates sheltered outdoor gathering space.*

**CENTRAL BUILDING**
EDUCATION
*The central building houses the exhibit barn and gathering space with views towards the poultry barns, as well as the teaching kitchen in the central core of the campus.*

*CLERESTORY WINDOWS FACING SOUTH*
*Provide passive ventilation in the summers and maximize direct sunlight in the winter.*

DORM | ARCHIVE | VISITOR'S CENTER | RESTAURANT | TEACHING KITCHEN | EVENT SPACE | EXHIBIT BARN

**TRANSPARENT FACADES**
*to maximize views for public programs*

**INTERNAL THROUGHFARES**
*Circulate people and light through all three buildings; reveals moments of interior programs*

**EXTENDED OVERHANGS**
*Provide shade for outdoor activities, classes, markets, and informal gatherings*

GOOD SHEPHERD POULTRY RANCH

# Mason Lane Farm

Goshen, Kentucky

In the long, multibay, bamboo-sided hay and truck barn at Mason Lane Farm, bales are stacked at each end and vehicles park in the middle. The shop and manager's office occupy another structure across the yard.

"Weed as a building facade: we love that idea!" says Eleanor Bingham Miller, owner of the diversified 1,985-acre Mason Lane Farm in the outer Bluegrass country of western Kentucky. She is referring not to marijuana but to Kentucky cane, the unusual material that Louisville architects Roberto De Leon and Ross Primmer used in the construction of her gable-roofed hay- and equipment-storage barn. Kentucky cane is a species of bamboo, which is itself a type of grass, and came from a nursery only thirty-five miles away, so the embodied energy cost of transporting it was minimal. Its use is part of an overall strategy to be as environmentally sensitive as possible in both building and planting.

The tall, hard, segmented bamboo canes are bundled in horizontal and vertical layers to form an eye-catching lattice. The open grid was employed partly for economy and partly for preserving the openness needed for air circulation, since the structure can hold up to four thousand hay bales. The simplicity of Kentucky's old tobacco barns, which often boasted large, louvered openings for air drying, provided inspiration. The architects point out a strong programmatic tie "in that the drying hay and the bamboo are both grasses at different scales, and both transform from green to gold through the drying process." And, as it happens, one of the experimental crops on Bingham Miller's farm—in addition to staples like corn, wheat, and soybeans—is hemp. The seeds are used in edibles for human consumption, CBD oil (cannabidiol) for pain management, and animal feed, and the fiber is used in textiles. To be clear, it's not the kind that brings on a high—though hemp is an identical plant to marijuana, it contains lower levels of the intoxicant THCA. As Bingham Miller exclaims vividly, she's "a serious multiyear licensed hemp farmer and not a pothead."

In addition to the bamboo-wrapped structure, Mason Lane Farm includes three grain silos and a gabled, metal-sided main barn containing an enclosed area for equipment storage, a large building maintenance bay, office, insulated work area and tool storage, kitchenette, shower, recycling area, and vehicle fueling station. The three structures border and shape a central gravel area—like an agricultural piazza—for the movement of large-scale farm equipment. The main barn uses ordinary materials in clever ways: for example, Homasote insulating wall boards (made of cellulose-based fiber) are exposed on the interior walls, like a sort of rustic paneling, and tool storage becomes another form of display. The goal, as De Leon says, "was to design a sustainable farm facility that conveyed a strong sense of place and site specificity" and to explore how sustainable design could be done without resorting to costly specialized systems.

The design of the complex, which has been widely celebrated in the architectural press, achieved a Leadership in Energy and Environmental Design (LEED) Silver certification through the use of primarily passive or low-tech and economical solutions. For example, water runoff was carefully considered to replenish aquifers. According to the architects, "The porous, drivable gravel surfaces are pitched to channel storm water

Bamboo, now weathered to gray, is the unusual material used for the open-air hay barn at Mason Lane Farm in Kentucky.

into two 'rain gardens' planted with native vegetation that provide additional wildlife habitat." Instead of roof gutters, which require maintenance, concrete "site gutters" on the ground under the roof eaves direct storm water to the collection basins. "In this way, the site and buildings work together as a large-scale integrated drainage system." A downpour during my visit showed how everything works: perfectly!

Mason Lane Farm is unusual not just for its architecture but for its overall ecological approach to the land. The property is going under a conservation easement to preserve the land in perpetuity for agricultural, recreation, wildlife, and conservation purposes. Today nearly three miles of farm frontage along Harrods Creek support freshwater mussels and otters. Bingham Miller says Wendell Berry, the Kentucky native, poet, agrarian philosopher, and farmer, was a major influence on her thinking. In his 2012 Jefferson Lecture at the Kennedy Center, titled "It All Turns on Affection," he lamented the increasing disconnect between humanity and the environment. He said, "I am nominating economy for an equal standing among the arts and humanities. I mean, not economics, but economy, the making of the human household upon the earth: the *arts* of adapting kindly the many human households to the earth's many ecosystems and human neighborhoods."

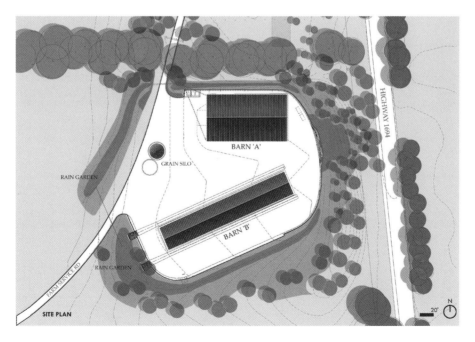

SITE PLAN

BARN 'A'

BARN 'B'

GRAIN SILO

RAIN GARDEN

RAIN GARDEN

FARM SERVICE RD

HIGHWAY 1694

20'

N

Interwoven
bamboo poles
help shelter
hay bales while
allowing air
circulation.
The adjacent
equipment
barn has metal
siding.

Bamboo geometry of the hay barn finds an echo in the corrugated metal siding of the equipment barn.

# Verdant Lawn Farm

Albemarle County, Virginia

The view from the main gate at Verdant Lawn Farm, off a two-lane road about twenty minutes west of Charlottesville, is enticing: through simple stone stanchions and diagonal wood braces, you can see the driveway winding left, up, and around a sloping cattle pasture—but then it disappears. You expect to see a landmark in the distance, but what you see is simply the land itself. And that is precisely the point, for according to the farm's landscape architect, Thomas Woltz of Nelson Byrd Woltz, based in Charlottesville and New York City, "The main drive is designed to create a powerful orienting experience, revealing viewsheds and narratives as one moves deeper into the site." The arcing geometry of the driveway acts as the literal and figurative story line for the farm, revealing each landscape and architectural event in sequence.

The owners of the 165-acre property, which had been mostly apple and peach orchards with a small dairy in two separate parcels, engaged NBW "to create a holistic master plan that established sustainable agricultural operations, designed the supporting farm infrastructure, and sited the future house and garden." In other words, NBW sought to provide a lens for understanding the landscape as a living ecological system. That meant mapping the contours, soils, plants, existing structures, and viewsheds west toward the Blue Ridge Mountains for a full ecological portrait and thinking about livestock—in this case, a two-hundred-head Angus cattle operation—as a maintenance tool. Also, because of problems with access to the property over a CSX freight rail line, the landscape architects were asked to create an alternative entrance—which became the stone gateway described above.

One of the farm's key landscape features is a bowl-shaped meadow rising to the left of the driveway toward the old dairy and silo. At the top of the hill stands a modest nineteenth-century farmhouse: the classic Piedmont Virginia farmstead. Farther along the drive is the new main house, sited by NBW but not designed by them, oriented toward the Blue Ridge Mountain panorama. The goal for the meadow was to preserve and enhance: remove invasive weeds, plant native switchgrass as a hay and forage crop, use rotational grazing (with the livestock acting as a maintenance tool), and, as firm associate Nathan Foley told me during a walk through it, generally take a curated approach to planting the grasses and perennials so they "stay low in the middle of the viewshed."

That understated but calculated and diligent approach has also been reflected in the repurposing of the dairy barn and silo as an event and party space as well as in the restoration of the farmhouse and the architecture of the new farm center, sited beside and taking visual cues from another existing barn. The new U-shaped barn, with gabled, standing-seam metal roofs and long monitor vents along two of the ridges, includes the board-and-batten-sided manager's house and open and enclosed storage and equipment sheds. It was built with large-dimension, long-span, locally harvested green oak. Below the manager's house is a distinctive chicken run, shaped like the

outline of one of the compound's wings but with screening for walls instead of wood panels. In all these ways, the new farm center seamlessly integrates with its setting, like a graft on an apple tree.

On my visit, Foley told me that one of the firm's heroes is the late Benjamin Howland, who taught at the University of Virginia after thirty years as a landscape architect for the National Park Service: he wanted design to feel inevitable. NBW design associate Jeff Aten sums up the team's approach: "The design goal is not to be invisible, but to accentuate the unique character and promise of Verdant Lawn."

The gateway bridge at Verdant Lawn Farm provides an enticing introduction to the unfolding agrarian landscape.

Angus cattle
gather in the
meadow below
the new central
complex at
Verdant Lawn
Farm, in Virginia.

1. Pasture
2. Screen planting
3. CSX railway
4. Main house & gardens
5. Guest house
6. Secondary entry
7. Dairy barn & silo
8. Central meadow
9. Farm center
10. Farm manager's house
11. Main entry gate
12. Steam buffer

Restoration is part of the landscape plan and includes an original gambrel-roofed barn and a white milking barn.

# Churchtown Dairy

Hudson, New York

"Cows don't like corners," says builder Rick Anderson as he talks about the grand round barn he designed and built for Abby Rockefeller at her biodynamic 250-acre Churchtown Dairy in Claverack, New York. Cows can get trapped in corners, especially when part of a herd. So Anderson crafted this remarkable four-story, eighty-foot-diameter domed structure, which resembles a cross between a circus big top and an amusement park carousel, or, as the quarterly *Edible Hudson Valley* headlined it, "A Castle for Cows." Ten sturdy, twenty-five-foot-tall yellow pine columns divide the space into pie-slice sections and rise through the circular hayloft all the way to the rafters and lantern, or cupola, which is festooned with Tibetan prayer flags. On the outside, bricks ring the base, rising to a band of windows, then a wall of vertical cypress boards painted white and the slate-tiled dome. Plexiglass tiles just below the cupola allow daylight to penetrate deep into the space. Cows are housed in the barn during winter months. When spring comes, the cows return to pasture, and the barn, once it has been cleaned, becomes an event space.

Inspired by historical structures like the 1908 Rebecca Rankin Round Barn in eastern Indiana, Churchtown's round barn anchors a three-hundred-foot line of connected buildings also designed or moved and reassembled by Anderson, including a cheese cave with a hand-crank elevator from the old Balsams Hotel in Dixville Notch, New Hampshire; an 1850s milking barn, also moved from New Hampshire; and a multidormered farmhouse used as the dairy's processing center, store, and office. Visible all at once from New York's Route 12, the entire complex glows milk-white above the meadow: an appropriately healthy—and sustainable—hallucination! Off to the right and slightly apart are the most recent additions: a small guesthouse, a greenhouse for medicinal plants, and a healing garden.

During the last century three families operated dairies on this land. But in the 1980s, with passage of the Food Security Act establishing a dairy herd buyout program and the price of milk declining, many small-scale farms, including the three here, folded. At the same time, farms were starting to be sold off to developers. That's when Peggy Rockefeller founded her American Farmland Trust and began purchasing farms to keep them from development, ultimately amassing three thousand acres in and around the Hudson Valley. Peggy died in 1996, and in 2008 her husband, David, began the process of turning the property over to their children.

Abby Rockefeller, their oldest daughter, requested the stand-alone parcel that became Churchtown. She told Anderson she wanted the dairy to be beautiful as well as sustainable, citing a favorite phrase from *A Handmade Life: In Search of Simplicity* by the influential wooden-yurt builder, teacher, and Maine native William Coperthwaite: "Beauty is a birthright, and where there is no beauty, there is great danger."

The twenty-eight dairy cows, including Brown Swiss, Jerseys, and Guernseys, live a good life here: morning and afternoon milkings are done as quietly as possible to create a soothing environment. Indeed, the historic milking barn feels like a devotional

space, with its ancient timbers framing a higher central "nave" as well as lower "side aisles" or cow stalls. Unlike many dairy farms, Churchtown keeps calves and their mothers together for the first five months after birth; the farmers gather plants from the garden to make an udder salve. Every day, they sweep the milking barn and scatter gypsum to absorb moisture. Chain-drive conveyor-belt gutters efficiently move manure and bedding material to the muck barn.

Abby Rockefeller founded Churchtown Dairy as part of her Foundation for Agricultural Integrity. One purpose is to bring people together "to work on the land in a way that is regenerative both for the land and the people working it. Farmers, cheesemakers, growers, carpenters, and administrators work together to create a whole farm organism, in which work, challenges, opportunities, and joys are shared." Production at Churchtown is not only raw milk, a little beef, medicinal herbs, and various cheeses, including cave-aged Camembert-style Churchtown Peggy (for Abby's mother) and mild and buttery Coperthwaite, named for the environmentalist, but also a vital and resonant sense of community.

At Churchtown Dairy, in New York's Hudson Valley, the great round winter barn resembles a carousel and dominates the assemblage of buildings.

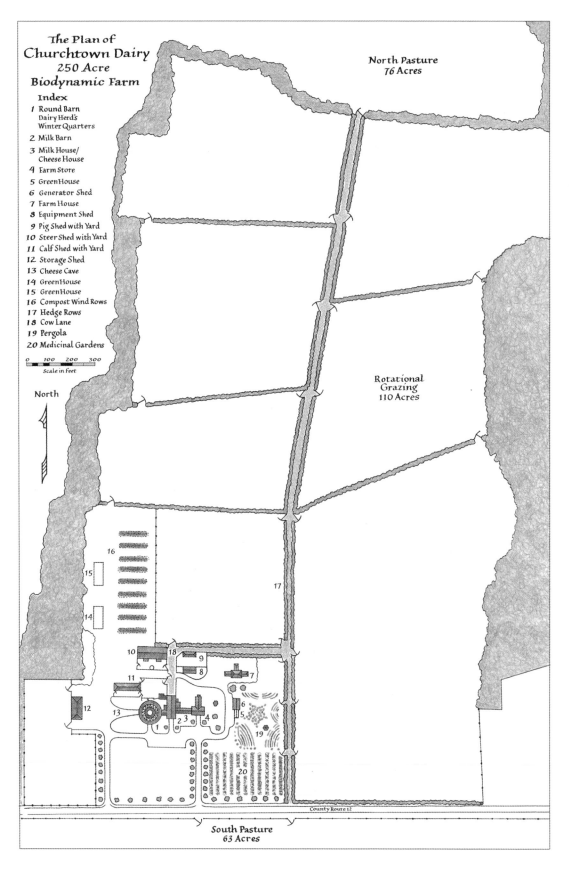

The Plan of
**Churchtown Dairy**
250 Acre
Biodynamic Farm

### Index

1 Round Barn
  Dairy Herd's
  Winter Quarters
2 Milk Barn
3 Milk House/
  Cheese House
4 Farm Store
5 GreenHouse
6 Generator Shed
7 Farm House
8 Equipment Shed
9 Pig Shed with Yard
10 Steer Shed with Yard
11 Calf Shed with Yard
12 Storage Shed
13 Cheese Cave
14 GreenHouse
15 GreenHouse
16 Compost Wind Rows
17 Hedge Rows
18 Cow Lane
19 Pergola
20 Medicinal Gardens

0   100   200   300
Scale in feet

North

North Pasture
76 Acres

Rotational
Grazing
110 Acres

County Route 12

South Pasture
63 Acres

The lineup includes a cheese cave beyond the stone arch at far left, milking barn at the center, and office/store to the right.

The interlocking timbers, tall columns, and triangular skylights of the double-decker round barn create a dramatic contrast to the classically rectilinear milking barn.

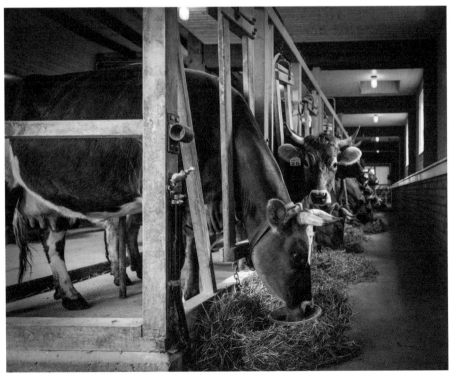

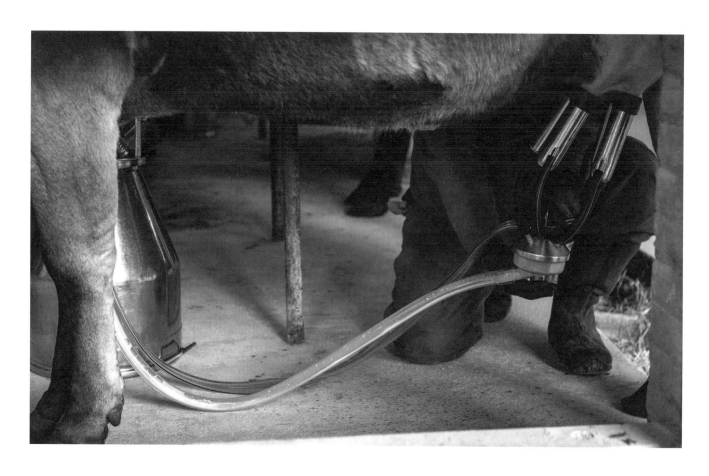

Two-way automation:
milking cups attach
to the teats; chain-
drive gutter carries
away the manure.

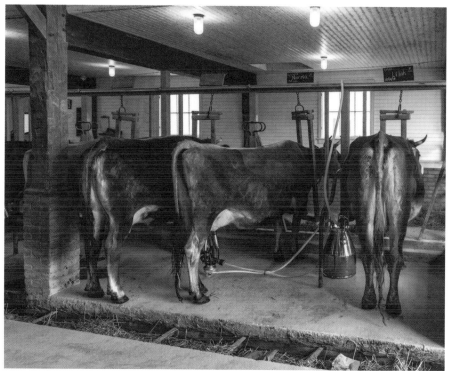

Little Ghent Farm

Ghent, New York

Recycled timbers on the store and in the farmhouse great room add a layer of history to what is a very contemporary complex. The main barn at Little Ghent Farm (previous spread) contains a rental apartment, to the left of the drive-through.

The story of Little Ghent Farm—chickens, laying hens, pigs, and honeybees—in the Hudson Valley, two hours north of Manhattan, is what inspired this book. It is the story of a successful British couple, Richard Beaven, an advertising executive and photographer, and Mimi Beaven, who had worked for a chef-restaurateur-author, deciding to step off the corporate ladder and into the barnyard because, as Richard says, "We felt it was important that we all know where food comes from."

Richard was transferred to New York sixteen years ago. The couple lived in suburban Scarsdale, and in 2005 they purchased a weekend house up the Hudson River near Ghent. Already interested in farm-fresh foods, they looked for local sources of eggs and meat, which led them to Lee and Georgia Ranney of Kinderhook Farm, where the cattle are grass fed and "they were just getting into sheep." Previously Mimi had attended agricultural college in Wales, so she knew something about the farming life. In 2012, when the Beavens' daughters were ten and twelve, they sold the house in Scarsdale and started looking for land to farm near their house in Ghent. They found this derelict seventy-five-acre farm no more than a mile away, but "the thirty acres of pasture were not pasture," says Richard. "In reality we had no idea what we had bought. Five fields with between five and twenty years of indigenous growth. Anything between weeds and first-stage forest prevailed." The existing structures, in various stages of decay, were essentially past saving, though some materials could be salvaged and recycled. "As we looked beyond the growth we discovered hidden magic everywhere and have done ever since: apple trees dotted in the hedgerows, fieldstone walls, a vernal pool in the woods, a meandering stream, ponds in the fields, patches of ramps, and shagbark hickory trees abundant with nuts."

It was a major leap into the unknown, but with encouragement and tips from friends like the Ranneys, the Beavens began. First, they hired builder Bill Stratton, whose custom residential building company is based in East Chatham, New York. Then a friend of the Beavens who was interning with Neil Pelone Architecture, in Troy, New York, connected them to Pelone. "They walked the land and were excited and open to collaboration and had some relevant experience," says Richard. Pelone's firm developed an agricultural master plan. It took roughly two years to clear and revive the pastures; the buildings were completed in 2015.

The architectural program is part commercial, part agricultural, and part residential and called for a commercial kitchen and store, a workshop and barn, and a house. Pelone and his associates came up with an ingenious three-part invention: three widely spaced but visually related contemporary gable-roofed, barnlike structures, each incorporating recycled barn wood for siding and each a riff on the idea of the rural building type known as a dogtrot: that is, two rooms separated by a breezeway. Nearest the road, on the left, is the structure with the public function: the store and the commercial kitchen, flanking a breezeway. Straight ahead and straddling the end of the entry road (which becomes the breezeway) is the barn and workshop, including a small apartment. Up the hill on the

right is the new house, overlooking the entire front field. At the center of its facade is a two-story window wall framing the entry (the third breezeway). The kitchen in the house can be used for cooking demonstrations. Essentially, each building has two uses, alluded to in the exterior treatments: one side
is rustic (vertical barn-wood boards) and the other modern (dark-stained vertical boards mounted flush). And the breezeway is treated in three ways: as a walk-through, a drive-through, and, metaphorically, a see-through.

Pelone explains how the house is a microcosm of the entire farm: "A number of distinct programmatic areas on the property lend themselves to specific sight lines from the house.... Different areas of the house cater to different areas of the parcel. The commercial areas around the house dictate the need to...see newly arriving customers and guests. The agricultural aspects lend themselves to pastoral views over animals and land, begging for perfectly framed views from the most leisurely areas of the home. The reality of a busy family life on a farm establishes very specific processional spaces into and out of the house: places to drop your boots, clean yourself off, and then enjoy the spoils of your labor."

Beyond the barn-workshop are a fixed-in-place winter chicken coop and two mobile chicken coops, which are essentially shed-roofed bungalows on the running gear of old hay wagons, allowing them to be moved across the pasture to rotate the foraging and spread the manure. There are up to 200 chickens raised for eggs and 150 for meat. In a delightful short film about the farm, Richard says: "While an animal is on the farm its life should be respected; it should be well cared for; it should be fed in as natural a way as possible.... If it's a chicken it's able to forage; if it is a pig it's able to hunt around and forage also." In other words, everything tastes better if the life that made the meal was natural and content. Richard sums up: "There can be few better rewards as a farmer than enjoying the food that you've grown yourself and seeing people learn about how their food is brought to the table."

Though the original buildings could not be saved, it was important to the Beavens that they recycle as much as possible, and the list of reclaimed and repurposed materials in addition to the barn siding is impressive, including roof timbers, doors, workbench, hardware, and windows in the winter chicken coop; the workbench in the barn shop; nesting boxes on the mobile chicken coops; the barn beams; and the beams and barn flooring for the dining table and as beams and interior accent walls in the house. The running gear, stone sink, and some of the lights in the kitchen and store were repurposed from off the farm. Of course, new materials also abound, like the oriented strand board (OSB) used in the house for maximum insulation to reduce energy use. One contemporary object caught my eye in the store beside the commercial kitchen: a contour map of Little Ghent Farm, made out of beautifully burnished, honey-toned wood. A gift from the architects, it captures the essence of this modern farm: an approach to the land that is pragmatic and artful and memorable.

Freshly baked bread is just one of the offerings at Little Ghent's farmstand kitchen.

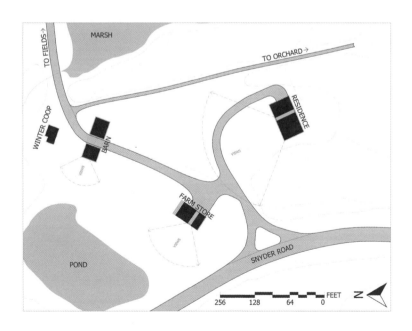

Designed as a kind of triple play, Little Ghent Farm consists of three similarly expressive metal-roofed buildings beside a central meadow. The farmstand kitchen is near the road. The barn with rental apartment occupies the far end of the meadow, and the house commands the hill.

MARSH

TO FIELDS →

TO ORCHARD →

WINTER COOP

BARN

RESIDENCE

VIEWS

VIEWS

FARM STORE

VIEWS

POND

SNYDER ROAD

FEET

256    128    64    0

N

# The Grey Barn and Farm

Chilmark, Massachusetts

The fifty grass-fed, mostly Dutch Belted cows at the Grey Barn and Farm, a certified organic, solar-powered dairy on Martha's Vineyard, are a bookish bunch. One of the award-winning cheeses they produce, with a little help from oil-trader-turned-farmer Eric Glasgow and his wife, Molly—is called Prufrock, after T. S. Eliot's famous poem "The Love Song of J. Alfred Prufrock," about the paralyzing anxiety of getting things wrong. Could the name for this "supple and stinky" cheese be a comment on the element of seasonal serendipity in the pastures where the cows turn grass into milk? Or simply about overcoming inertia and the fear of leaping into an entirely new line of work? Another cheese is called Eidolon, inspired by Walt Whitman's poem "Eidólons." The word, from the Greek, means an idealized person or thing—in this case a "bloomy-rind" cheese. Molly says it is "a word that can describe the miraculous melding of elements that creates a taste of place." A third cheese, with the more prosaic name of Bluebird, is a well-marbled blue. The Glasgows also raise pigs, chickens, and sheep.

Eric showed me around the farm and told me their story as he removed twenty dozen eggs from a walk-in refrigerator beside the cheese cave. He graduated with a BA in economics from the University of Chicago, where he helped pay his way through college by cooking in restaurants and baking baguettes. He first worked for the brokerage Dean Witter in their commodities research department. After it merged with Morgan Stanley, he moved to the energy and commodities company Vitol. Molly studied design and was an art director in New York and London, then a stay-at-home mom for their two young sons. Their first lettuce and herb garden, in Connecticut, had made them think about food and where it came from. Then in 2007 Eric was transferred to London, where they lived in Hampstead and had a vegetable garden, finding inspiration in the pervasive "local food movement." And every day Molly shopped for the family's food directly from the sources—farmers, dairies, fish and meat mongers, and bakeries. This new experience was a contrast to the ubiquitous grocery store and a model she and Eric were interested in pursuing themselves. In 2008, said Eric, "we had lots of discussion about when we would move back to the States and where would we go...long-term planning became 'why not now?'" Plus, they wanted the boys, who had not yet attended a US school, to get a little "Americanness." They had vacationed on Martha's Vineyard, and it was where their extended families enjoyed coming together. Eric took a six-month leave from work, and then "this farm came up and we got excited about turning it back into a working dairy."

There was a lot to do, with several decrepit structures to be removed. They worked with Gregory Ehrman of Hutker Architects (Vineyard Haven, Falmouth, and Boston) and landscape architect Kris Horiuchi, of Horiuchi & Solien Landscape Architects in Falmouth, to preserve one big barn and design a new milking barn and creamery, main house, and sunken vegetable garden. The architects had not designed a farm before, so there was a learning curve for everyone. For example, on sixty acres of pasture, they could have no more than sixty milking cows. The agricultural preserve—the pastures

Grey Barn and Farm is a dairy on Martha's Vineyard that provides eggs as well as milk and cheese in a new/old compound divided by beautiful long walls of boulders.

Boulder wall separates farmstead from residence. The living room windows become monumental landscape paintings.

and barns—needed to be separate from the five-acre lot for the new house. The milking barn/creamery had to be on high ground for drainage, "and when it rains it's still a mess," says Eric. And the Glasgows wanted the new architecture to be esthetically pleasing.

The result is a vivid, environmentally sensitive design that uses axial vistas and paths to tie together the farmstead shop, stately old barn, new creamery and milking barn, sunken garden, and house. A low wall of dry-stacked boulders forms the central axis. It skirts the edge of the sunken garden by the old barn and runs all the way up the gentle slope to the creamery, marking the path between them and tethering the structures to each other and to the landscape. The creamery and the milking room occupy opposite ends of the long, horizontal, one-story shingled barn. The milking parlor is what is known as a parallel type, meaning that the cows stand parallel to one another. Designed by Rolf Reisgies and built by Richard Handfield, it allows the cows to be inside for as short a time as possible. The raw milk is then pumped over the drive-through at the center to the creamery side.

On the cross axis, near the old shingled barn, now used as a bakery over the basement cheese cave, is a rectangular sunken garden behind walls of concrete to keep the herbs and espaliered quince and apricot out of the wind. Pathway steps nearby are recycled granite curbing. Farther along this same cross axis is the residential precinct, marked off by another low boulder wall. The driveway passes through a gate and enters a gravel courtyard. In Europe, Eric and Molly had found inspiration in the architectural books of Beta-Plus Publishing, especially a "Belgian minimalist farmhouse." According to the architect, the new two-story timbered and gabled house, with garage in a side wing, "is designed to resemble an old barn converted for modern living." Giant barn doors slide across huge contemporary window walls to open dramatic views of the cows in their pasture: those elegant bovine belts turn every vista into a painting.

On the farm's website Molly writes: "Most days are still learning days. Learning about the effects of snow, learning about weird mold in the cheese cave—the list goes on and on. Is it worth it? Did we make the right decision? Are we still crazy? Yes, yes, and yes." Now I think I understand the poetic names for those first two cheeses. After a big decision like changing your lifestyle, you tend to rethink it now and again, and an idealized life needs work to support it. Nature must be nurtured. The phrase "a taste of place" epitomizes not only the cheeses of the Grey Barn and Farm but the entire complex. The design is at once site specific and visually delicious. And who knows what the cows will be reading next!

The cheese is washed and set in the creamery. In another barn nearby, the Katahdin sheep contemplate their good fortune in finding Grey Barn and Farm.

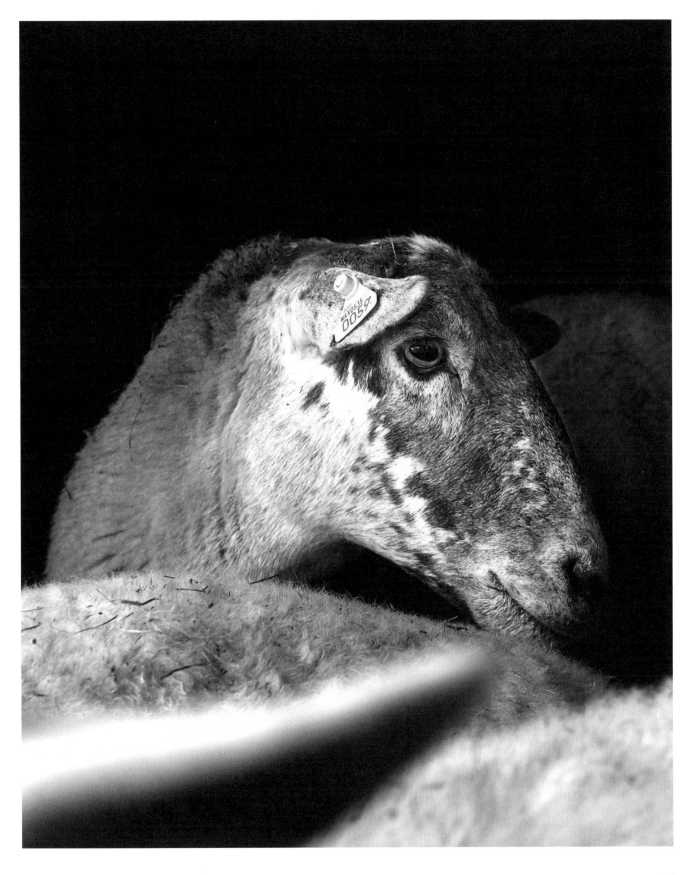

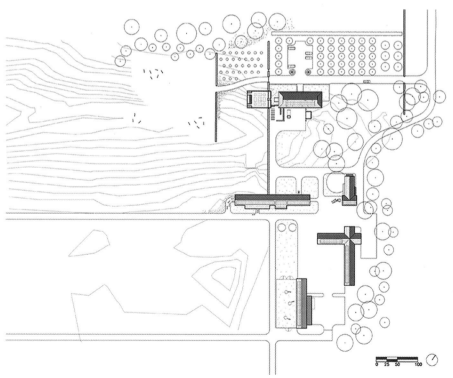

The site plan of Grey Barn and Farm shows how the barns line up along the boulder walls. Molly and Eric's house is not shown but sits at the end of the driveway on the top far left of the drawing.

0  25  50    100

# Prugger Farm

Rasen-Antholz, South Tyrol, Italy

In the Dolomites, the rugged mountain range that straddles the Austria–Italy border, steep, forested slopes meet luxuriant grassland along the valley floors. The road and railway tunnels, bridges, and towering peaks recall European travel posters from the 1920s. I drove south from Innsbruck, first along the fast and efficient autobahn and then on a winding two-lane road into the agricultural Val Pusteria, to the picturesque village of Rasen-Antholz, a collection of mostly traditional wood-and-stucco chalets. I was looking for the farm of Thomas Prugger, who owns the local lumber company, but I missed the turnoff and had to ask for directions at a local hotel. The proprietor said in perfect English, "The Prugger farm? That very modern building? Go back to the main road and turn right onto the driveway by the apple stand." And there it was, behind an imposing square barn, which Prugger later told me dated from the Napoleonic era. The farmhouse is a dramatic modern cube that was designed by Innsbruck architect Reinhard Madritsch, of Madritsch Pfurtscheller, to function both as the Pruggers' home and as the barn to support their small herd of Scottish Highland cattle. Wrapped in darkly weathered vertical wood strips, the three-story structure is set against a hill overlooking a wide pasture.

The driveway splits at the corner of the three-story structure: turn right for access to the bottom level and the stable, now holding farm equipment. Turn left and proceed partway up the slope to the entry on the middle floor, consisting of an L-shaped living-dining-kitchen zone that wraps around the hayloft. The top floor holds three bedrooms, a wide play hall, and a ramp leading up to a roof deck that's hidden within the rectangular parapet. The cubist outline, wide window walls, open spans, and rooftop ramp bring to mind a modern icon like Le Corbusier's 1930 Villa Savoye, near Paris. This barn-house is its country cousin—not just a "machine for living," as in Le Corbusier's famous phrase, but a "machine for living and farming." Interior walls alternate between stone and eye-catching, horizontally layered recycled timbers.

The twenty-one-acre farm—five acres of pasture and sixteen of forest—grows potatoes and apples. Until recently the cattle grazed in the adjacent field. Prugger, a hang glider in his free time, has a very direct and no-nonsense approach to the farm. As he was showing me the hayloft, I asked him where the cattle were. With wry under-statement, he said, "The cattle are in there," pointing to the freezer. The pasturing didn't work out as they had planned, but at least there was beef for the winter!

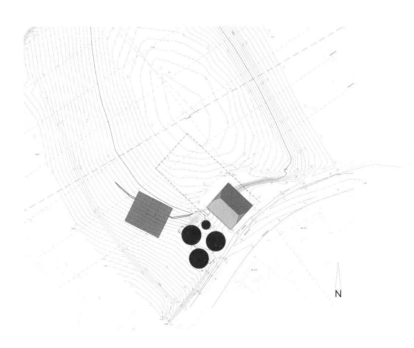

The cattle barn is also the house at contemporary and cubic Prugger Farm in the Dolomites of northern Italy. You pass the gabled Napoleonic barn to get to the house.

N

The area is historically important, which affected the siting; for example, on the little hill behind the house is a Mussolini-era bunker, where the children like to play. The existing farm buildings were too dilapidated to be saved, so starting over was necessary. Prugger and Madritsch wanted to build a structure that would quietly and closely fit into the landscape as a single element and not signal its use to the outside world. The resulting simple, geometric design draws inspiration from the big square Napoleonic barn across the driveway. You can make out the stable's vehicle entrances at the bottom and the wide window wall in the living room on the floor above, but from a distance the building reads as a single unit. The topography helps separate living and working, with the kitchen-dining area opening to outdoor living space on the hillside, away from the lower-level entrance to the stable. For another approach to combining functions in a single structure, compare this design to Oosterhout Farm, described in a later chapter.

Highland cattle used to call this modern farm home. Though wrapped in a contemporary package, the design is age-old: the stable digs into the hill at the bottom, while the floors above contain the living areas. At the top is a roof deck camouflaged within the building's parapet, like a twenty-first-century battlement.

# Schönenberg Farm

Basel, Switzerland

Georg Schmid is a Swiss architect and co-owner, with Johannes Feld and Jonas Wuest, of F.A.B. – Forschungs- und Architekturbüro (Research and Architecture Office), based in Basel. Schmid's farm, just outside the city, has been in his family since the 1930s and is the site for a remarkable new cow barn that F.A.B. designed. He explains, "As we are not farmers, we leased some of the property to farmers. Around the millennium we had to reevaluate the farm's orientation. Along with that came the plan to redesign a part of it and to build a new cow barn, to be used for milk production." And then there was the notion that if they had to spend money on a barn to increase milk production, "Why not a nice barn?"

When I arrived at F.A.B.'s courtyard office in a residential section of Basel on a foggy fall day, Schmid's partners, Feld and Wuest, gave me a quick introduction to the firm before driving me out to the farm. I learned that Schmid had held an internship with the internationally known Swiss firm Herzog & de Meuron, and that the three partners are fans of Charles and Ray Eames, whose midcentury-modern furniture is permanently on display at the Vitra Design Museum (incidentally, designed by Herzog & de Meuron) in Weil am Rhein, Germany, just over the border on the outskirts of Basel. One Eamesian tenet that seems especially relevant to F.A.B.'s work is "Design depends largely on constraints."

The constraints in this case were their goals "to create an ensemble with the existing buildings" on the sloping site without obscuring the view of the historic farmhouse and to embed a new twenty-one-thousand-square-foot barn for seventy cows in a steep hill "so that it would seem to be part of the landscape, in spite of the large volume/program."

They worked with professional barn builders, adapted their techniques, and ultimately reinvented the idea of a barn. The attenuated shed shifts axis as it follows the contours of the land and, thanks to the spreading eaves of the shallow-gable sod roof, almost disappears into the slope, especially as seen from the apple orchard down the hill; as Schmid says, the "same grass as on the surrounding meadows creates a kind of mimicry." In a particularly ingenious twist, the exterior walls are not walls but screens consisting of the tall trunks of hazel trees woven together and embedded in the concrete perimeter wall. Why hazel? The trees are indigenous and found throughout the farm—naturally!

I asked if any historical or contemporary buildings had an influence on the design of the barn. The reply was that the surrounding nature, the landscape and flora, were the key influences, but "not without including the industrial character of agricultural constructions." The architects have deconstructed key features of the landscape and artfully recombined them: cow barn as enlarged hedgerow! Two tall milk silos in gleaming stainless steel act as a vertical counterpoint, drawing the eye and confirming that this is not just another "artificial pasture" but an industrial building. Steel posts and engineered beams permit a floating roof and wide-open interior that allow everyone to see the cows being milked. It was feeding time when I walked through, and the inhabitants seemed contented, though perhaps unaware of their environmentally avant-garde setting. Even though the building takes its cues from nature, it has a strong architectural presence (a pleasing contradiction), making it a vivid exemplar of a modern approach to farm design.

Gustav Mahler's "Das Lied von der Erde" ("The Song of the Earth") comes to mind at the sight of the cow barn at Georg Schmid's farm near Basel: the walls of trees and roof of grass appear more landscape than structure. Only the gleaming milk silos add an industrial note.

The dairy barn at Schönenberg Farm blends into its hillside site with a sod roof and hazel branches for walls.

# Oosterhout Farm

Rijswijk, The Netherlands

The abstracted gable form of Oosterhout Farm at Rijswijk, south of Amsterdam, combines sheep barn, skylit atrium, and loft-like in-law apartment. Compare Oosterhout Farm to Prugger Farm: both are contemporary approaches to housing people and animals in the same structure.

Marc Oosterhout is a cofounder of the major Dutch advertising firm N=5, who, with his wife, Margot, decided to shift lifestyle gears and move with their two sons and two daughters from a busy, status-conscious commuter suburb of Amsterdam to the farming community of Rijswijk, known for producing fruit juices and jams. He still goes to Amsterdam regularly but mostly works from home. What inspired such a big change? Marc told me, as Margot handed me a glass of delicious homemade apple juice: "The nature around us. The change of seasons. And all the different activities that come with living in the country: keeping sheep (using the wool for clothing), cultivating vegetables, chopping wood. We were looking for something new—for a quiet place with a lot of space and freedom to live."

I found a related call to freedom and change in N=5's video campaign for the Dutch national rail network NS: It's a Saturday. A young man walks out the door of his home, plugs in earphones and listens to Billy Joel's "Piano Man" as he bikes to the train station to catch the 9:00 a.m. to Haarlem, and then Rotterdam. In Rotterdam he is about to leave the station when he sees that the London train is about to depart and on the spur of the moment decides to take it. At St Pancras International Station, he grabs a cab to a nightclub called Ricky's Piano Bar, where he joins part of the audience in singing along with the musician, who, of course, is in the middle of that very tune. The simple and effective branding line for the campaign is "Where do you want to go today?"

Marc and Margot wanted to go to the country and wound up with a historic 12.8-acre farm with apple, walnut, and pear orchards, grassland, and a house. He recounts, "The last thirty years, the property was owned by a sculptor. The house was treated well, but the surroundings weren't. The garden was a mess, and the property was full of ugly buildings. First, we started to refurbish the garden. We built a greenhouse to cultivate vegetables, and we created a kitchen garden. After a few years we decided to replace the old buildings with the new barn, where we combined a lot of different activities. We created an apartment for extra living space to study and write. The barn inspires us to live our life of freedom."

That barn, designed by Ivar van der Zwan, of Workshop Architecten, is both contemporary and historical and had to be reviewed by the Rijksmonumenten board (the cultural heritage council). It's a simple, crisp solar-paneled gable (they wanted to live off the grid) supported on timber trusses, with an exterior covered in vertical Douglas fir siding stained black. It's sited along the north–south axis of the house, just behind it, and divided into three zones: hayloft and sheep pen; central plexiglass-roofed atrium rising the full height of the building for use as a winter garden and workshop; and, on the south end, closest to the house, a two-story apartment. The light-filled atrium opens to views on the cross axis through the barn to an orchard on the southwest and pasture on the northeast. The apartment functions as overflow for guests and as Marc's study; perhaps in the future, it will become an in-law unit for Margot's mother. Details add to the clarity of the design: the horizontal exterior nailing pattern decisively reinforces the barn's geometric outline.

Walnuts, pears, apples, and prunes are grown in the fields around the original house and modern barn.

I met van der Zwan at his loft office in Amsterdam, where he explained the design: "The old, black wooden barns (the wood was covered with tar as a preservative) that used to be common in the Dutch countryside were a major influence. And we matched the height of the gutter and the ridge of the roof exactly with an adjacent historical fruit shed. The sheep and the old fruit trees determined the positioning of the barn and the windows and doors. And the large number of solar panels were very influential in the final outcome. First, we had to find matte black ones in order to create the traditional black look. The specific size of the solar panels determined the final dimensions of the barn. Exactly half of the roof consists of solar panels. We tried to design them in such a way that they are one with the building, instead of placed on top of it." Indeed, the solar panels seamlessly extend the line of the roof, and they are numerous enough to make the entire farm energy-independent.

I mentioned to van der Zwan that in the abstracted barn shape I saw echoes of buildings like William Turnbull's 1960s Binker Barn houses at the Sea Ranch in California (noted in the introduction), and he said he had long been an admirer of that residential development but that he also found inspiration in the houses of Frank Lloyd Wright and especially the 1914 Villa Henny by early modern Dutch architect Robert van't Hoff.

On the day I visited the Oosterhouts, a classic Morris Mini was being rebuilt by one of their sons in the winter garden and the sheep were grazing in the field, companionably accompanied by the family's black cat. And though I arrived by car and not by train, I felt inspired. Marc is one of the authors of an important book in Dutch on branding and is now at work on another, to be published in English this time. Perhaps he'll call it *Where Do You Want to Farm Today?*

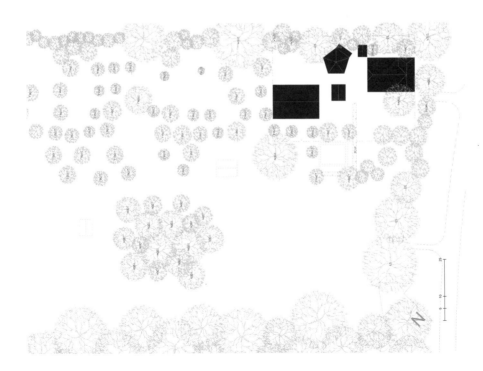

At night the "winter garden" at the center of the new barn, which is set back from the road and behind the historic house, glows like a large lantern.

# Terre Bleu

Campbellville, Ontario, Canada

In the summer of 2018, more than 55,000 enthusiastic visitors swarmed through the rustic modern breezeway and into the fields at Terre Bleu, Ontario's largest organic lavender farm, forty minutes west of Toronto in rural Milton. Such early success was a surprise to the owners, Ian and Isabelle Baird, who moved here in 2011 and opened the 160-acre farm to the public only three years ago. I met Ian on a rainy day in November, and he led me on a fast-paced tour through the operation as he told me how they got here.

Like several other stories in this book, the founding of Terre Bleu involved a big lifestyle change. Ian is from a large family in Newfoundland. His father was a farmer. A business and science graduate of Memorial University there, Ian became publisher of a daily newspaper before being headhunted to Toronto and climbing the executive ladder at EMC, a major computer data storage company (now part of Dell). He spent most of his time traveling the globe. In Germany he saw an ad for the Ontario property, which was then just hayfields with a horse barn and an unfinished house.

He says, "We bought the property to make a change from our urban lifestyle in downtown Toronto to a rural, sustainable farm lifestyle that would allow us to try a new farm type and give our children a chance to grow up more outdoors, discovering the world around them." Isabelle is a physiotherapist and part-time hospital manager who had been an Olympic triathlete, so the outdoor life was especially important to her. She now bicycles to a hospital nearby in the town of Guelph.

But what kind of farm to start? They had previously fallen in love with a lavender farm while vacationing in Quebec. They liked the diversity of the ecosystems on this property, including centuries-old cedar and mixed forest, wetlands, streams, and low, rolling hills. And the soil was good for lavender growing. So Ian, a self-styled "tech-preneur," set about designing the brand and the building himself, after doing a computer search for modern barns.

The gateway building was a special challenge. Commanding a hill at the entrance to the property, it's a tall, gabled barn with a breezeway between the store and the processing plant. The breezeway leads to a deck running the length of the structure and frames dramatic views across the rows of lavender, which were laid out for visual appeal and "so visitors could walk through the fields." Indeed, the lavender is planted on axis with the entry barn, so the barn acts as a monumental doorway into these walkable rows of fragrance.

Ian worked with a local contractor to achieve his architectural idea. "I was inspired by designs that were minimalist in nature and have a Scandinavian feel," he explains. The city initially denied him a building permit because "the design was integrated between the two uses, therefore the key element of the design—a continuous roofline—was not getting approval. We fought long and hard and eventually won." Clad in vertical wood strips, like enlarged battens, the building has a pleasing texture resembling architectural corduroy, a vertical echo of the horizontal rows of forty thousand plants spreading out below.

The enterprise is increasingly complicated, with four distinct businesses: the farm, the tourist attraction, the retail store (selling products onsite and online), and the manufacturing business (they make 65 percent of the products they sell). The lavender grown here is distilled or crushed or ground or used whole to make everything from lavender chocolate truffles and lavender maple syrup to lavender bath soaks and lavender green tea (which I recommend). The Bairds also grow sunflowers and have an apiary for harvesting honey, and they work with local small businesses like soap makers and bakeries. Here, lavender isn't just a commodity: it's also a learning experience: the farm offers guided tours, yoga sessions, art walks, and special events.

Ian says, "I used to run a billion-dollar business, and this is much more stressful." But, clearly, he enjoys it as he enthusiastically describes the harvest process: "We do it artisanally—with scissors, with fifty university students. We call them ambassadors; they lead tours and deal with the public as summer jobs. A lot have graduated in animal science or are in the last year of doing a master's degree. They become very invested in the program. They learn from it, and we learn from them."

One day the Bairds placed a yellow door in the middle of a field as an art project. Now it is a permanent popular attraction drawing long lines—a smaller reprise of the farm's grand breezeway entrance. The Bairds' daughter, Madeline, came up with the saying that is inscribed on the frame: "Walk through the door, your worries behind you, your joys are ahead." Just add lavender...

The modern barn at Terre Bleu, west of Toronto, functions as storage center, office, product shop, and eye-catching gateway to the lavender fields.

At Terre Bleu, the copper distillery vessels are gleaming sculptural objects in their own right and form a key element in the parklike landscape somewhat apart from the main entrance barn.

The barn's observation deck floats above the orderly rows of lavender. Paths lead into the forest, to the distillery, and to more fields.

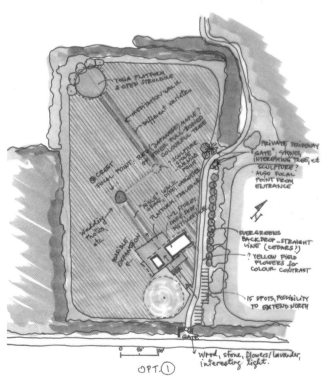

# Crackenback Stables

Thredbo, New South Wales, Australia

Call it a stable with stature. Horses and people share the contemporary compound at Crackenback, in Australia's Snowy Mountains.

In the 1982 film *The Man from Snowy River*, about horse wrangling and young romance in the Australian high country, there is a remarkable scene of the hero riding his buckskin horse down a nearly vertical mountainside, in what is called the "terrible descent." Crackenback Stables, combining living quarters, horse barn, and equipment shed wrapped in panels of rusted steel and angled sheets of corrugated iron, is the modern-day architectural equivalent of such a ride. Built on a hundred-acre alpine site near Thredbo, a ski center in the remote Snowy Mountains halfway between Sydney and Melbourne, it was designed by Rob Brown of Casey Brown Architecture for John Fielding, who founded Bellevarde Constructions, an unusually design-oriented residential builder. Crackenback is both daring and direct. The leap is in the way tough industrial materials shape and seat a sculptural modern farm.

Fielding, who began his career in Canberra as a bricklayer, started his company in 1980 to pursue his longtime interest in innovative architect-designed houses. He finds inspiration in "simple buildings built from economical materials that are finely detailed and maintenance free, also architect-designed buildings that are appropriate for their locations." Clearly, he enjoys the imaginative process and found a kindred spirit in Brown.

Here's how Brown describes developing the design with Fielding: "We talked about sheds and what an Australian shed might be and decided we had an opportunity to reimagine this iconic form in a modern way—simply and with no pretense. Following some initial sketches from John that were literally on a napkin, I started with a circular design that drew on the form of the hacienda. This evolved into one long building with a hole at one end that, a few lunches later, finally became two separate pavilions, still with a hole in the middle. Having a covered, large arrival area where you could drive or ride up to the buildings and unload was an important element that came through from the very early drafts. John liked the idea of using simple materials, and with a little refinement we turned this into wrapping the building in a corrugated skin. The final materials would be concrete [for the hydronically heated slab], rusted steel, and corrugated iron, true staples of any great Australian shed."

The longer of the two buildings places the self-contained two-bedroom living space for Fielding and his wife, Sherry, and recessed veranda above the stable (containing five stalls, tack room, feed room, and workshop), and tapers to a one-story farm manager's residence across the covered entry. That portal is also used for saddling up, storing firewood, and unpacking a car. Set perpendicular to the stable block—partly to shield the stable and living quarters from the wind—is an equipment shed. The corrugated iron skin of both buildings follows the lines of their shallow gables to emphasize the structures' trapezoidal form.

Rusted steel panels and corrugated metal siding under what is essentially an elongated shed add to the strong industrial character of Crackenback, helping it withstand the remote and rugged landscape.

With no eaves and the wraparound skin, along with concealed and protected gutters to direct rainwater to storage tanks, the design offers a defense against the harsh climate. As Brown vividly explains, "To deal with life in the Snowies, the stables would need to cope with freezing winds and snow as well as summer bushfires. The final form is organic, gutterless, and animallike. It hunkers into the ground to escape the attention of the elements." Or, like that exceptional Snowy River horseman, Crackenback rides out extremes of heat and cold with innate skill and contemporary, even cinematic, panache.

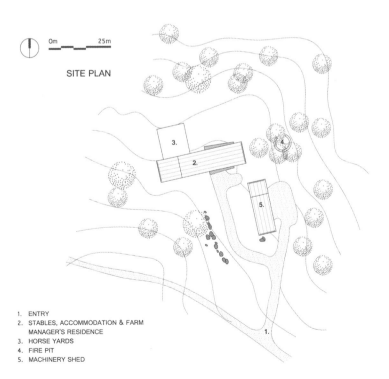

Inside, a simple
material palette
continues: concrete,
wood, steel.
The window wall
echoes the shelving
opposite while
framing views out
across the treetops.

Om ___ 25m

SITE PLAN

1. ENTRY
2. STABLES, ACCOMMODATION & FARM
   MANAGER'S RESIDENCE
3. HORSE YARDS
4. FIRE PIT
5. MACHINERY SHED

The distinctively
angled roof of
the barn (the
darkest rectangle
on the plan) at
Swallowfield Farm,
south of Vancouver,
British Columbia,
adds new energy
to a traditional
shape. Upstairs
is a hayloft and
gathering space for
poetry readings;
animal pens and
equipment storage
are below.

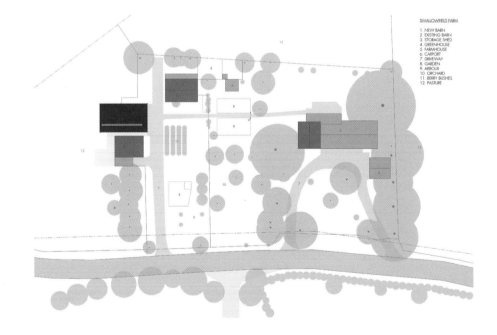

SWALLOWFIELD FARM

1. NEW BARN
2. EXISTING BARN
3. STORAGE SHED
4. GREENHOUSE
5. FARMHOUSE
6. CARPORT
7. DRIVEWAY
8. GARDEN
9. ARBOUR
10. ORCHARD
11. BERRY BUSHES
12. PASTURE

The power went out just before I arrived during a downpour at Jenny and Dennis deGroot's five-acre Swallowfield Farm, in berry and horse country an hour southeast of Vancouver. But that did not dim the enthusiasm of their welcome, and, indeed, it showed off a key characteristic of the barn complex designed by their architect son, Asher: ample daylighting thanks to window walls at opposite ends of the loft and a grand skylight running the length of the roof gable. The two-story barn, oriented east–west for morning and evening light, boasts a distinctive profile. Asher aptly describes the roof line as "off-kilter." The gable itself forms a right angle, and one side of the barn is higher than the other. Eaves and side walls project beyond the building to form a welcoming entrance porch. The building is situated near other outbuildings a few hundred feet beyond the deGroots' ranch house. Visible from the road, with hay storage and poetry readings occurring on the second floor (the bales do double duty as bleacher seating) and wood shop and animal stalls below, the new barn has become a celebrated local landmark.

Here's how Dennis, a retired high-school administrator, and Jenny, an assistant principal and teacher at a local elementary school, describe how this farm came about: "We had just lost our previous farm to the encroachment of large subdivisions and were looking for a place that would be free of that encroachment within the Agricultural Land Reserve [a protected area administered by British Columbia's Agricultural Land Commission]. This property also bordered a large, protected green space, and we wanted someplace where we could continue raising our four boys, with lots of places to wander and explore. It turned out that Swallowfield was all of that and more. It now has become that for our grandchildren. There were several outbuildings on the property, and we always had deep regrets that the hundred-year-old barn on our last property had been demolished. We wanted somehow to replace that. We were used to holding large gatherings of people in that barn." Hence the idea that their new barn should have a community aspect.

"We love to grow, preserve, and eat good food. That means spending years making good topsoil for pastures and gardens. That has been deeply satisfying. We also raise several beef cows each year as well as pigs for our own pork and broilers for our own freezer and eggs for ourselves and whoever comes by at the right time."

As teachers, the deGroots especially value the educational aspects of the farm. "To see a cow birth a calf just across the fence in the field is a miracle to be shared. It is also great to bring someone along on the process of slaughtering chickens that will end up on the dinner table. Not an easy thing to do, but very important. It's a teaching place for those who are interested in learning." It was handy, then, that one of their sons turned out to be an architect who could design what might be called the deGroots' ultimate classroom.

Asher explains the design and its construction: "One of the biggest challenges for me came from the reality that I was also the contractor and builder for the project.

Guests enter the hayloft by an interior stair; hay bales are hoisted up through the double doors at the rear of the barn.

Every detail needed to be one that I could build myself—not one I could pass off on some other trade." Financial constraints also dictated a creative approach. For example, the barn's cladding is reclaimed concrete board forms sourced from a project that a cousin was working on. The construction was a contemporary version of a classic barn raising, with lots of help from family and friends, as Asher recalls: "It was the first year of my practice, and everyone helped out in construction. One Saturday there were thirty-five people working." They had a pig roast after they raised the walls. The moment frame required extra expertise for the LVL (laminated veneer lumber) beams, so Asher tapped into the barter economy: the engineering fee for the barn was a pig (for slaughter). But his engineer friend could not fit a whole pig in his freezer, so they "still owe him something."

The deGroot farm is named Swallowfield after the place where Jenny was born on Vancouver Island and for the swallows that were already on this property. The new barn combines continuity with innovation as both a working farm structure and a community center. It's both recognizable and architecturally surprising. Asher says he enjoys "finding materials and forms that fit a context without replicating exactly the historical forms. I hope that this barn is of its place and time."

As I was leaving, Jenny offered me a jar of her blackberry jam, but I declined, saying it would be confiscated at customs. She responded wryly, "Yes, they have a lot of my jam." It had stopped raining. I drove away, admiring how this remarkable family expresses their strong commitment to the land.

The striking angle of the roof, the exposed beams, and filtered light create a celebratory space for community get-togethers, not just for silage.

The front of the
barn is on axis with
the garden path
and offers a wide
welcome to animals
and people.

# Waterview

North Bruny Island,
Tasmania, Australia

Bruny Island is at the southern tip of Tasmania, 386 miles across Bass Strait from mainland Australia. This rugged coastal environment is where Melbourne architect John Wardle maintains Waterview, a 1,087-acre ranch with 1,500 to 2,000 sheep. I asked what drew him to this place: "I had a schoolteacher who made a great impression on me. We stayed in touch over the years, and when he retired to Bruny Island, my wife, Susan, and I visited his property and were captivated by the natural beauty and lifestyle. Waterview had been on the market for five years before we bought it, and we saw it as an opportunity to restore and invest in something to last. We use the farm as an antidote to our hectic lives in Melbourne, Victoria." It also functions as a kind of maker's laboratory. One three-day retreat for his architectural firm resulted in, among other farm-related structures, a delightful wooden, wing-shaped observation platform overlooking the ocean.

The Wardles purchased the property in 2002 and spent the next ten years improving the condition of the land and planting more than six thousand indigenous trees. The farm dates to the 1820s, and its first owner, Tasmanian merchant Captain James Kelly, built the original cottage. The Wardles used the cottage as their main dwelling while figuring out what to add or update. Two existing wooden structures—one now used for farm equipment and one for shearing the sheep—line the driveway. The wool is sold to local (and occasionally international) mills.

In 2012 the Wardles built the Shearers' Quarters on the site of the old shearing shed, which had burned down in the 1980s. This remarkable new structure—built to accommodate shearers during the annual wool harvest as well as family, friends, and work colleagues on holidays, retreats, and planting weekends—resembles an angular periscope laid on its side. Following the contours of the sloping site, an attenuated shed roof morphs into a spreading gable to frame expansive vistas of grazing sheep and rocky coastline.

John explains, "It was designed as a reimagined shed. Local timbers and the archetypal lean-to and gable profiles were the starting point, to which a sculptural lens was applied. The building's geometry shifts in both plan and section, transforming from a slender single pitch in the west, housing bedrooms and bunk rooms, and slowly expanding into a broad gable for the living spaces and coastal view. This exploration of these two primary agricultural structures allows the plan to align exactly with both the fall of the land to the south and the line of the original cottage to the north."

In 2015 they started work on the old cottage, stripping away previous additions to reveal the original structure while adding a new living area between the kitchen and bedrooms. The layered soffits and exposed rafters of the original house are continued in the addition. John says, "In revealing the original structure, many stories and building techniques were discovered, and these informed the rebuild." The original veranda also provided inspiration and "extends and encapsulates the new works, tying new and old together." Waterview is itself an accretion of layers, from the restored and expanded

Captain Kelly's Cottage, dating from the early nineteenth century, where John Wardle has artfully exposed aspects of its construction history, to the adjacent geometric twenty-first-century shed architecture of the Shearers' Quarters to the simple shearing shacks some distance away.

That dialogue between old and new is vividly expressed in a time-lapse animation created by filmmakers Coco and Maximilian. Without human figures but syncopated to a disarmingly simple score, it gives a sense of what it's like to be at Waterview. Shutters, cabinets, and doors open and close; dining-table candles snuff out as if a meal has just ended; a herd of sheep passes by; and then the slanting light deepens into the moon's reflection over the sea. I am relaxed and refreshed by this display—and completely mesmerized. It is the modern farm as dreamscape, the ultimate balm for busy urbanites.

Captain Kelly's Cottage commands the knoll, while the shearers' shed sits somewhat behind, along the entry road. Sheep graze the surrounding fields.

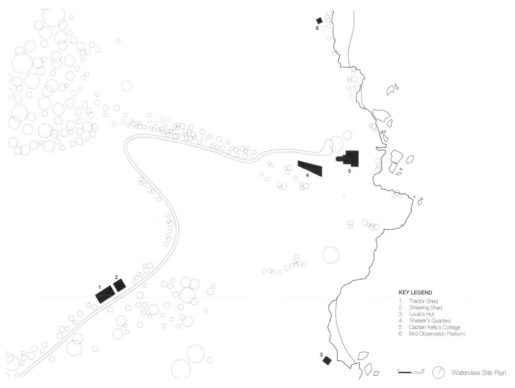

KEY LEGEND

1. Tractor Shed
2. Shearing Shed
3. Louis's Hut
4. Shearer's Quarters
5. Captain Kelly's Cottage
6. Bird Observation Platform

Waterview Site Plan

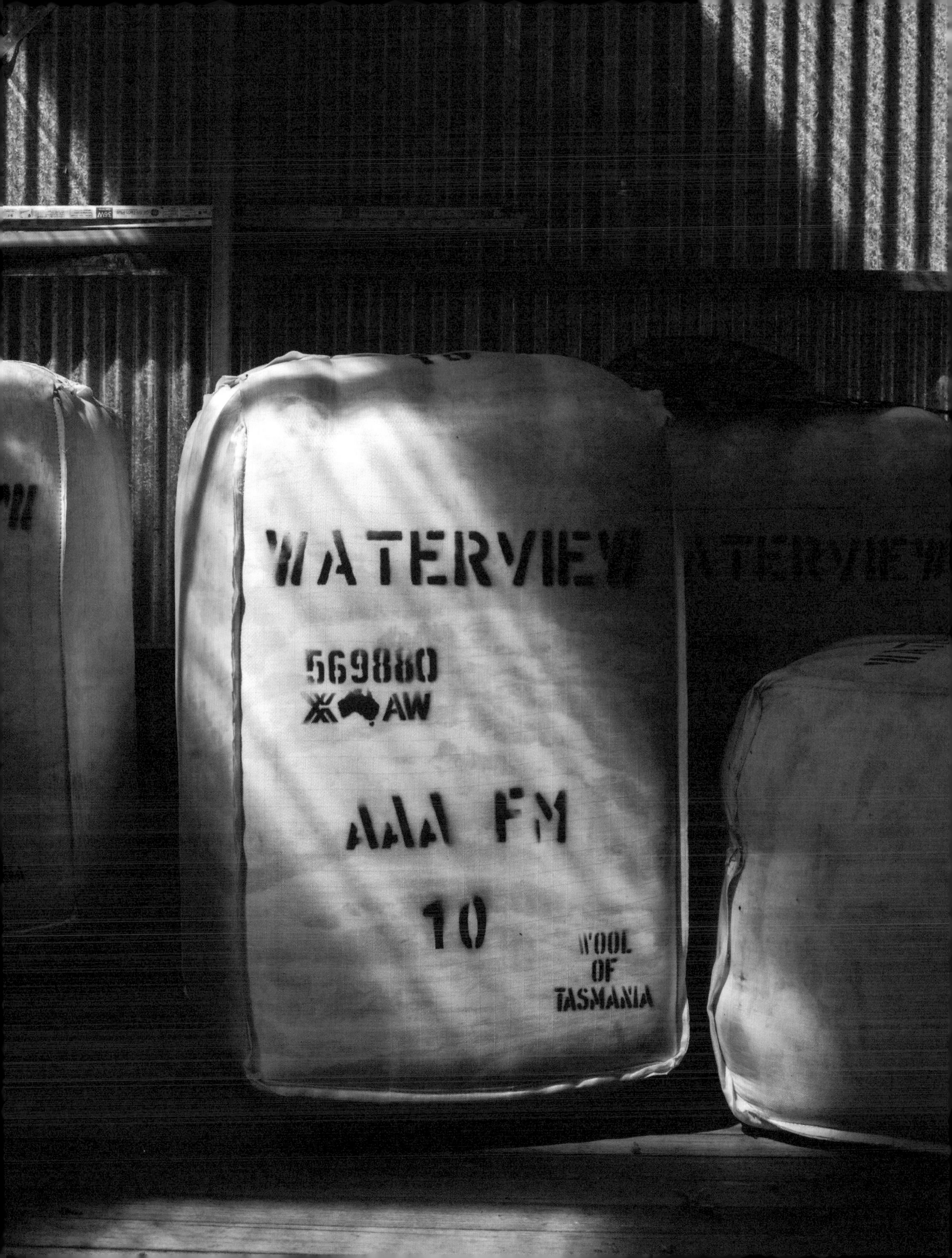
WATERVIEW
569880
AW
AAA FM
10
WOOL
OF
TASMANIA

The wool harvest is just part of the story at Waterview. The architecture weaves together structure and site, history and modernity, past and present.

# McEvoy Ranch

West Marin County, California

Memory and serendipity played important roles in the development of McEvoy Ranch. In 1990, when Nan Tucker McEvoy was seventy-one, she purchased a 550-acre "broken-down dairy ranch" in the rolling hills of western Marin County, a fifty-minute drive north of her home in San Francisco. At the time, she chaired the board of the Chronicle Publishing Company, which included the *San Francisco Chronicle*, the newspaper founded by her grandfather. As a girl she had spent summers riding, fishing, and exploring the gardens at her family's ranch on the Rogue River in southern Oregon. The ranch was submerged behind a flood control dam in the 1970s. Nan wanted her grandchildren to have the same opportunities for outdoor freedom that she had known; the ranch would be a retreat. However, as interior designer Michael Booth recalls, "She (like her son) was not one to lie around a pool. It required a purpose, which grew over time."

But the ranch was in bad shape: some buildings had collapsed or were on the verge of doing so. McEvoy recalled in a brief memoir that one structure was in such bad shape that she asked the local fire department if they "would like to set it ablaze for a practice session. They responded with enthusiasm." Because of the agricultural zoning, in order to make any improvements she had to come up with a bona fide agricultural use. Booth says, "She never liked the notion of herding cattle unless they were medium rare (same with sheep)." Northern California's Mediterranean climate was great for wine grapes, but the region was already heavily planted in grapes. Olives were a possibility: McEvoy liked olive oil, the climate worked for olives, and she could be first in the planting of olives instead of last in the long line of grape growers.

Inspired by Maggie Blyth Klein's *The Feast of the Olive*, a history of olives and olive oil making, McEvoy flew to Italy to meet one of Klein's advisers, olive and wine expert Maurizio Castelli, "and came home with one thousand baby Tuscan olive trees." Castelli helped her establish a nursery for propagating and selling olive trees. He remains a consultant to the ranch today, according to ranch president Samantha Dorsey, who explained the operation to me. The ranch includes fifty-seven acres of Tuscan olives for certified-organic extra virgin olive oil, along with orchards and a huge kitchen garden for the making of jams, marmalades, tapenades, and honey, and more recently has broadened into ten acres of Pinot Noir, Syrah, Montepulciano, and Refosco grapes. Everything is sustainably grown and harvested.

The heart of McEvoy Ranch is a small valley hidden from the gate along the Point Reyes–Petaluma Road. In addition to some refurbished barns, new structures were needed "for living, for guests, for entertaining all [McEvoy's] hoped-for olive oil buyers," and for the olive press, which would include the ranch shop and business offices. The ensemble is the decade-long work of a multifaceted team of artists including Michael Booth, architect Marc Appleton, landscape designer Patrick Brennan, rock mason George Gonzalez, and contractor Russ Morita.

The olive mill building designed by Appleton sits somewhat apart from the other buildings and first can be spotted from the driveway. A wraparound veranda by the ranch

At McEvoy Ranch, one of the original barns has been restored as a plant nursery for the extensive kitchen garden. After driving up the winding road, you come to the "Bunny Gate," the entrance to the heart of the operation.

shop offers views across one of the small lakes. The tall oil vats and imported Rapanelli olive milling equipment occupy a hall at the rear. Farther down the driveway and clustered around a stone-paved, bamboo-bordered piazza are a country kitchen, rebuilt Victorian house, and the wonderfully exotic Chinese-inspired entertaining pavilion above a grand oval pool overlooking another pond. Highly crafted Mount Lassen lava rock walls—recalling Incan masonry in their precision—tie everything together.

Working with McEvoy was a great joy, according to Appleton, because "we were all kind of part of the family." Indeed, Appleton had gotten to know McEvoy as the longtime friend of his mother. The two women had met in the early 1960s, when McEvoy was helping run the Peace Corps. They had kept in touch ever since. The design team always met and ate in the country kitchen at the ranch. "She couldn't read plans and had no patience for methodical planning, which was initially challenging, but after a while we just went with it," adds Appleton. Discussions often involved showing her an idea, and "if it appealed to Nan, she'd just say 'Do it.'"

Indeed, a spontaneous and often whimsical quality is evident, from the meandering stone walls and pathways to the use of the native skink lizard (a favorite of McEvoy's grandchildren) as the ranch logo. A sculptural skink even climbs the copper roof of the pagoda-like entertaining pavilion. Marc says her generosity and joy in building things was infectious and inspired everyone around her. "We all tried, often unsuccessfully, just to keep a sense of order. It was a delightful journey."

Nan McEvoy died in 2015 at ninety-five, but her ranch thrives. In that brief memoir, she wrote: "Last but not least, my grandchildren adore the ranch, as I had hoped they would. Becoming an olive grower turned out to be a sterling idea."

Porches and elaborate stone paths and stairways invite resting and rambling. The extensive grounds include a serene egg-shaped swimming pool beside one of several shimmering ponds.

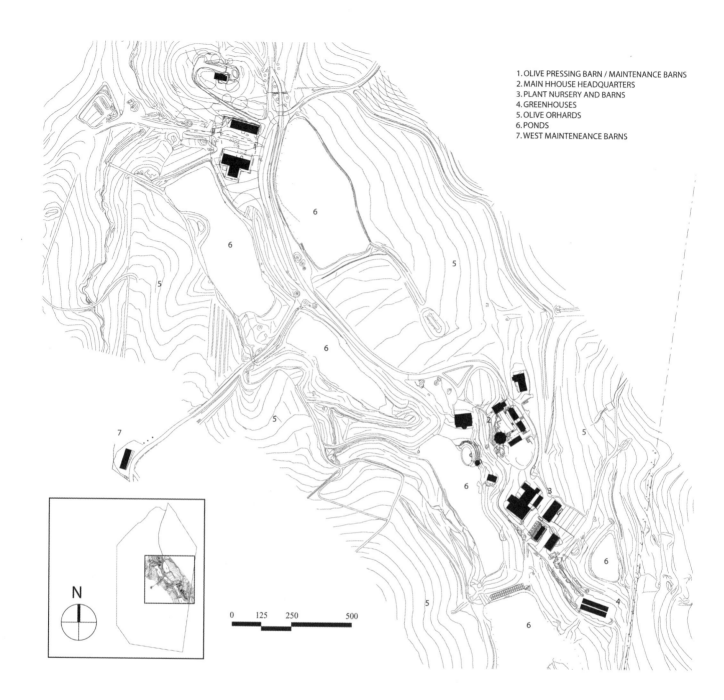

1. OLIVE PRESSING BARN / MAINTENANCE BARNS
2. MAIN HHOUSE HEADQUARTERS
3. PLANT NURSERY AND BARNS
4. GREENHOUSES
5. OLIVE ORHARDS
6. PONDS
7. WEST MAINTENEANCE BARNS

N

0    125    250         500

The site plan
shows how the
olive orchards and
ponds surround
the visitor center
and olive pressing
barn, upper left,
and the main house
headquarters,
lower right.

The gleaming Rapanelli olive press commands attention, or rather, "Attenzione!"

# ACKNOWLEDGMENTS

Perhaps the examples in this book do not make a trend, but I can begin to see a pattern: many of the modern farmers I met in the United States, Canada, Europe, and Australia came to the land from other walks of life. Often they were looking for new adventures, a healthier, more eco-friendly lifestyle, or simply a way to show their children where ham and eggs come from. In some cases, the farmer is just doing what comes naturally: for example, Frank Reese has always loved poultry. He is determined to preserve and study original strains and has even founded an institute to expand on this work.

As I toured these farms, I was reminded of a quotation inscribed on classically inspired Hilgard Hall at the University of California at Berkeley, designed by campus architect John Galen Howard to house the School of Agriculture and completed in 1917. It reads: "To Rescue for Human Society the Native Values of Rural Life." That, in essence, is what all of the families in this book are doing, with the help of innovative contemporary architects. I am hugely grateful to all the client/architect teams for their generosity in welcoming a stranger, for sharing their stories, and for enthusiastically showing me the new farm.

I owe so much to the vision, drive, and professionalism of Jan Hartman, acquisitions editor at Princeton Architectural Press, who entrusted me with this topic in the first place and then deftly guided its progress to completion. Her enthusiasm is contagious. I owe additional thanks to PAP editorial assistant Stephanie Holstein, fresh out of Kenyon College, who created spreadsheets and managed queries and photo requests with efficiency and panache. Editor extraordinaire Sara Stemen patiently parsed every paragraph, making sure my words made sense. My wife, Mary, read the essays and, as always, clarified my thinking, not to mention my prose. I dedicate this book to her, and to the memory of our parents, Evey and Jack, and Mimi and Charlie, who always knew what a farm could be.

# APPENDIX:
# THE FARMS

At Virginia's
Verdant Lawn
Farm, an old silo
is preserved as
sculpture

Introduction

| 16 | GREGORY FARM | Santa Cruz Mountains, California<br>*Not open to the public* | William Wurster |
| 17 | HAYSTACK MOUNTAIN SCHOOL OF CRAFTS | 89 Haystack School Drive<br>Deer Isle, Maine 04627<br>(207) 348-2306<br>haystack-mtn.org | Edward Larrabee Barnes |
| 17 | SEA RANCH | 975 Annapolis Road<br>Annapolis, California 95412<br>(707) 785-2444<br>tsra.org | Joseph Esherick<br>MLTW Architects (Charles Moore, Donlyn Lyndon, William Turnbull Jr., and Richard Whitaker)<br>Lawrence Halprin |
| 19 | CAKEBREAD CELLARS | 8300 St. Helena Hwy<br>Rutherford, California<br>(800) 588-0298 | William Turnbull |
| 19 | ISLAND DESIGN ASSEMBLY | Penobscot Bay, Maine<br>islanddesignassembly.org | McLeod Kredell Architects, Middlebury, Vermont<br>mcleodkredell.com |
| 21 | HAY BARN | Somis, California<br>*Not open to the public* | Zoltan E. Pali, FAIA, founder of SPF:a<br>Los Angeles, California<br>spfa.com |
| 21 | TRACTOR SHED | Elk Valley, Oregon<br>*Not open to the public* | Fieldwork Design & Architecture<br>Portland, Oregon<br>fieldworkdesign.net |
| 22 | STONE BARNS CENTER FOR FOOD & AGRICULTURE | 630 Bedford Road<br>Pocantico Hills, New York<br>(914) 366-6200<br>stonebarnscenter.org | Machado Silvetti Architects<br>New York, New York<br>machado-silvetti.com<br>Asfour Guzy Architects<br>New York, New York<br>asfourguzy.com |
| 27 | CHILTERN BARNS | Buckinghamshire, England<br>*Not open to the public* | McLean Quinlan<br>London and Winchester, England<br>mcleanquinlan.com |
| 29 | MARTIN'S LANE WINERY | Kelowna, British Columbia<br>martinslanewinery.com<br>*Not open to the public* | Olson Kundig Architects<br>Seattle, Washington<br>olsonkundig.com |

Featured Farms

| | | | |
|---|---|---|---|
| 32 | SOTER VINEYARDS, MINERAL SPRINGS RANCH | Mineral Springs Ranch 10880 NE Mineral Springs Road Carlton, Oregon 97111 (503) 662-5600 sotervineyards.com | Backen & Gillam Architects St. Helena, Sausalito, and Beverly Hills, California bgarch.com |
| 42 | SNUCK FARM | Pleasant Grove, Utah (801) 318-8448 snuckfarm.com *Not open to the public, except for classes* | Lloyd Architects Salt Lake City, Utah lloyd-arch.com Louise Hill, Architectural Designer Salt Lake City, Utah louisehilldesign.com |
| 52 | GOOD SHEPHERD POULTRY RANCH | Lindsborg, Kansas goodshepherdpoultryranch.com *Not open to the public* | Design of the Good Shepherd Institute: MASS Design Group Boston, Massachusetts massdesigngroup.org |
| 58 | MASON LANE FARM | Goshen, Kentucky *Not open to the public* | De Leon & Primmer Architecture Workshop Louisville, Kentucky deleon-primmer.com |
| 66 | VERDANT LAWN FARM | Albemarle County, Virginia *Not open to the public* | Nelson Byrd Woltz Landscape Architects Charlottesville, Virginia New York, New York Houston, Texas nbwla.com |
| 76 | CHURCHTOWN DAIRY | 357 County Route 12 Hudson, New York 12534 (518) 851-2042 churchtowndairy.org | Richard Anderson sapodillabay@gmail.com |
| 88 | LITTLE GHENT FARM | 282 Snyder Road Ghent, New York 12075 (518) 392-0804 madeinghent.com | Neil Pelone Architecture Troy, New York nparch.com |
| 98 | THE GREY BARN AND FARM | 22 South Road Chilmark, Martha's Vineyard, Massachusetts 02535 (508) 645-4854 thegreybarnandfarm.com | Hutker Architects Martha's Vineyard, Falmouth, and Boston, Massachusetts hutkerarchitects.com |

| | | | |
|---|---|---|---|
| 110 | PRUGGER FARM | Rasen-Antholz, Val Pusteria, Italy<br>*Not open to the public* | Architect Reinhard Madritsch,<br>Madritsch + Pfurtscheller<br>Innsbruck, Austria<br>madritschpfurtscheller.at |
| 120 | SCHÖNENBERG FARM | Basel, Switzerland<br>*Not open to the public* | F.A.B. – Research and Architecture Office<br>Basel, Switzerland<br>fab.ch |
| 126 | OOSTERHOUT FARM | Rijswijk, The Netherlands<br>*Not open to the public* | Ivar van der Zwan, Architect,<br>Workshop<br>Amsterdam, The Netherlands<br>workshop.archi |
| 134 | TERRE BLEU | 2501, Sideroad 25<br>Campbellville, Milton, Ontario<br>(519) 512-0522<br>terrebleu.ca | Ian Baird and John Vanderwoerd,<br>Vanderwoerd Drafting & Design<br>Arthur, Ontario<br>ontariohomedesign.ca |
| 142 | CRACKENBACK STABLES | Thredbo, New South Wales, Australia<br>*Not open to the public* | Casey Brown Architecture<br>Sydney, Australia<br>caseybrown.com.au |
| 154 | SWALLOWFIELD FARM | Fort Langley, British Columbia<br>*Not open to the public* | Asher DeGroot,<br>Motiv Architects Inc.<br>Vancouver, British Columbia<br>motivarchitects.com |
| 164 | WATERVIEW | Bruny Island, Tasmania, Australia<br>*Not open to the public* | John Wardle Architects<br>Melbourne, Australia<br>johnwardlearchitects.com |
| 174 | MCEVOY RANCH | 5935 Red Hill Road<br>Petaluma, California 94952<br>(866) 617-6779<br>mcevoyranch.com | Appleton Partners LLP –<br>Architects<br>Santa Monica and Santa Barbara, California<br>appleton-architects.com<br>BAMO<br>San Francisco, California<br>bamo.com |

Daniel P. Gregory is a longtime magazine and website editor and author of *Cliff May and the Modern Ranch House*. He graduated from Yale, received his PhD in architectural history from UC Berkeley, and lives in the Bay Area.

Abby Rockefeller is the founder of the Churchtown Dairy.

Published by
Princeton Architectural Press
202 Warren Street
Hudson, New York 12534
www.papress.com

Editor: Sara Stemen
Designer: Benjamin English

Library of Congress Cataloging-in-Publication Data
Names: Gregory, Daniel Platt, author.
Title: The new farm : contemporary rural architecture / Daniel P. Gregory.
Description: Hudson, New York : Princeton Architectural Press, 2020. | Summary: "The New Farm" delves into fourteen farms across America, Europe and Australia to portray the reinvention of traditions for today's contemporary design and organic farming"—Provided by publisher.
Identifiers: LCCN 2019036736 (print) | LCCN 2019036737 (ebook) | ISBN 9781616898144 (hardcover) | ISBN 9781616898144 (epub)
Subjects: LCSH: Farm buildings. | Farm buildings—Pictorial works. | Architecture, Modern—21st century—Themes, motives. | Architecture, Modern—21st century—Pictorial works.
Classification: LCC NA8200 .G74 2020 (print) | LCC NA8200 (ebook) | DDC 725/.3700222—dc23
LC record available at
  https://lccn.loc.gov/2019036736
LC ebook record available at
  https://lccn.loc.gov/2019036737

Image credits
p. 2–3: Courtesy of Terre Bleu Lavender Farm. 4–5: Adrian W M Jones. 6–7: Rob Brown, courtesy of Casey Brown Architecture. 8–9: Courtesy of Workshop Architecten. 16: William Wurster, Environmental Design Archives, UC Berkeley. 17: Edward Larrabee Barnes, the Museum of Modern Art / licensed by SCALA and Art Resource, New York; courtesy of the Frances Loeb Library. Harvard University Graduate School of Design. 18 top: Morley Baer, ©The Morley Baer Photography Trust, Santa Fe. All reproduction rights reserved. Used by permission. 18 bottom and 19: William Turnbull, Environmental Design Archives, UC Berkeley. 20–22: Island Design Assembly. 23: John Linden. 24: Brian Walker Lee, courtesy of Fieldwork Design & Architecture. 25 top: Michael Moran / OTTO. 25 bottom: Courtesy of Machado Silvetti Architects. 26: Ben Hider. 27–28: Will Scott, courtesy of McLean Quinlan. 30: James O'Mara. 31: Nic Lehoux. 32–33, 34 (top): David Papazian, courtesy of Soter Vineyards. 34 bottom: Jim Pipkin, courtesy of Soter Vineyards. 36: Hallie Whyte, courtesy of Soter Vineyards. 37: Courtesy of Backen & Gillam Architects. 38–41: David Papazian, courtesy of Soter Vineyards. 42–43, 45: Mark Weinberg. 46 top: Elisha Braithwaite, courtesy of Snuck Farm. 46 bottom: Courtesy of Lloyd Architects. 47–49: Mark Weinberg. 50: Elisha Braithwaite, courtesy of Snuck Farm. 51: Christine Armbruster, courtesy of Snuck Farm. 52–54, 56: Jim Richardson. 57: Courtesy of MASS Design Group. 58–60: Courtesy of de Leon & Primmer Architecture Workshop. 62: Daniel P. Gregory. 63–65: Courtesy of de Leon & Primmer Architecture Workshop. 66–67: Courtesy of Nelson Byrd Woltz Landscape Architects. 69: Eric Piasecki / OTTO. 70–71: Courtesy of Nelson Byrd Woltz Landscape Architects. 72: Eric Piasecki / OTTO. 73 top: Courtesy of Nelson Byrd Woltz Landscape Architects. 73 bottom, 74–75: Eric Piasecki / OTTO. 76–77, 79: Marc Bryan-Brown, courtesy of Churchtown Dairy. 80: Courtesy of Rick Anderson. 81 top: Marc Bryan-Brown, courtesy of Churchtown Dairy. 81 bottom: Georgia Landman, courtesy of Churchtown Dairy. 82–84, 85 top: Marc Bryan-Brown, courtesy of Churchtown Dairy. 85 bottom, 86–87: Georgia Landman, courtesy of Churchtown Dairy. 88–89, 90 top: Don Crossland. 90 bottom, 93 top: Courtesy of Neil Pelone Architecture. 93 bottom: Don Crossland. 94–97: Courtesy of Neil Pelone Architecture. 98–99, 101: Molly Glasgow, courtesy of Grey Barn and Farm. 102: Eric Roth. 104–8, 109 top: Molly Glasgow, courtesy of Grey Barn and Farm. 109 bottom: Courtesy of Hutker Architects. 110–11, 113 top: Retter Wolfgang, courtesy of Madritsch Pfurtscheller. 113 bottom: Courtesy of Madritsch Pfurtscheller. 114–18, 119 top: Retter Wolfgang, courtesy of Madritsch Pfurtscheller. 119 bottom: Courtesy of Thomas Prugger. 120–21, 123, 124 top: Christian Baur and Serge Hasenböhler, courtesy of F.A.B.–Forschungs- und Architekturbüro. 124 bottom: Courtesy of F.A.B.–Forschungs- und Architekturbüro. 125: Christian Baur and Serge Hasenböhler, courtesy of F.A.B.–Forschungs- und Architekturbüro. 126–28, 130–33: Courtesy of Workshop Architecten. 134–35, 137–43: Courtesy of Terre Bleu Lavender Farm. 144–45: Rhys Holland, courtesy of Casey Brown Architecture. 146, 148: Carly Martin, courtesy of Casey Brown Architecture. 149–52: Rhys Holland, courtesy of Casey Brown Architecture. 153 top: Carly Martin, courtesy of Casey Brown Architecture. 153 bottom: Courtesy of Casey Brown Architecture. 154–55, 156 top: Ema Peter. 156 bottom: Courtesy of Motiv Architects. 158–63: Ema Peter. 164–65: Trevor Mein. 167, 168 top: Chris Crerar. 168 bottom: Courtesy of John Wardle Architects. 169: Chris Crerar. 170–71: Trevor Mein. 172: Chris Crerar. 173 top: Trevor Mein. 173 bottom: Chris Crerar. 174–75, 177–78: Ali Harper, courtesy of McEvoy Ranch. 179: Alex Vertikoff. 180–81: Ali Harper Photography, courtesy of McEvoy Ranch. 182: Courtesy of Marc Appleton. 183 top: Ali Harper Photography, courtesy of McEvoy Ranch. 183 bottom: Alex Vertikoff. 184–85: Courtesy of McEvoy Ranch. 186: Daniel P. Gregory. 188: Eric Piasecki / OTTO